KU-111-543

ACKNOWLEDGMENTS

Our thanks go to the stall holders who volunteered information, gave advice and were willing to be photographed for this book. Our editor, Abigail Willis, also deserves special thanks for her patience and diligence over the year it has taken to research this book.

HOW TO USE THIS BOOK

The last edition of The London Market Guide was subdivided into categories which caused some confusion for readers. In this second edition we have simplified things by listing the markets alphabetically. If you want to find the markets in your area simply refer to the map at the beginning of the book and use the contents page as the map index. Another change has been the removal of the car boot sales section from this edition because they change so quickly. If you do want up-to-date information about car boot sales look out for our new website www.london-bargains.com which should be online shortly.

ICON INDEX

 antiques

 clothing

 books

 shoes

 fruit & veg

 household goods

 cut flower & plants

 fresh meat

 cloth

 furniture

 fresh fish

 cafés & restaurants

 towels & bedding

 bric-a-brac

 fresh bread

 music (CD's etc)

 pubs

 electrical goods

 fresh coffee

 toys

 produce

 toiletries

 hardware

 pet supplies

 arts & crafts

 haberdashery

CONTENTS

Church Street Market

INTRODUCTION

Visiting a street market in London is not just a way of stocking up on cheap socks, or shaving off the pennies on a bunch of spinach – it's an experience in itself. I'll avoid getting too philosophical in the space of a brief introduction, but I will say that all the markets we've visited in the course of researching this book have made a clear impression. Perhaps it was the sky on a particular day, or a passing comment from one of the traders or punters, or some wonderful oddity pulled out of a tangled box of unpromising tat. Of course, not all the experiences we've had have been positive, but far better the occasional cross word or duff piece of fruit than the sterile predictability of a supermarket – when did you last have a really memorable experience in the canned vegetable aisle at Sainsbury's?

Since the last edition of this book was published, there have been a few disheartening developments: the end of Farringdon Book Market and Earl's Court Sunday Market, as well as the decline of some smaller venues such as Exmouth Market. One encouraging change in recent years is the growth in the farmers market phenomenon, which has given new life to places like Borough Market and Camden Passage, and offered hope to small producers who have had little to smile about in recent years.

Things change far more quickly than a person involved in the writing of guide books would like, and I have to accept that the delicious fruit observed on page 53 has been eaten, and that the 50's shirt I noted on page 115 has probably already done more than a few stints on the Hoxton bar scene – the beauty is in the details, but details change. No review can cover everything, but I hope when you're thinking about a trip to one of London's street markets, this book can give you an idea of what to expect – we've taken trouble to try and capture the atmosphere of each place.

If you were to rely on the media to form your opinions, you might be given to thinking that we will all soon be shopping via the internet, and that markets – and maybe even shops – will one day be a thing of the past. Hopefully when you flick through this book, and visit some of the markets, this projection will be shown to be as false as it is inhuman. Markets are not only a place where money can be exchanged for goods, they are a place to meet, a space for public expression. Far better a group of stalls under a London sky than individuals stuck in front of computers, ordering items from an ugly and distant warehouse, without a word being spoken or a glance exchanged.

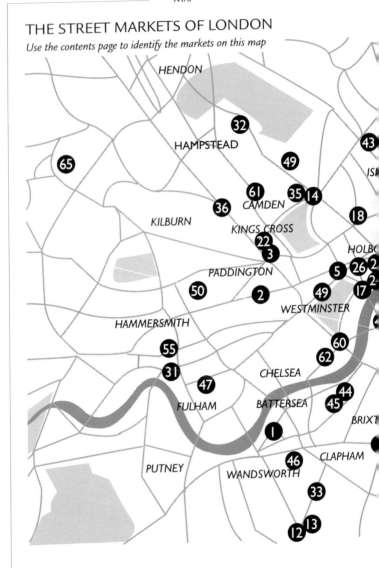

THE STREET MARKETS OF LONDON
Use the contents page to identify the markets on this map

HENDON

32

HAMPSTEAD

49

43

65

IS

61 **35** **14**

36 CAMDEN

KILBURN

KINGS CROSS

18

22

3

HOLB

PADDINGTON

5 **26** **2**

50

2

17

49

WESTMINSTER

HAMMERSMITH

60

55

62

31

CHELSEA

47

44

FULHAM

BATTERSEA

45

BRIXT

1

46

CLAPHAM

PUTNEY

WANDSWORTH

33

12 **13**

42

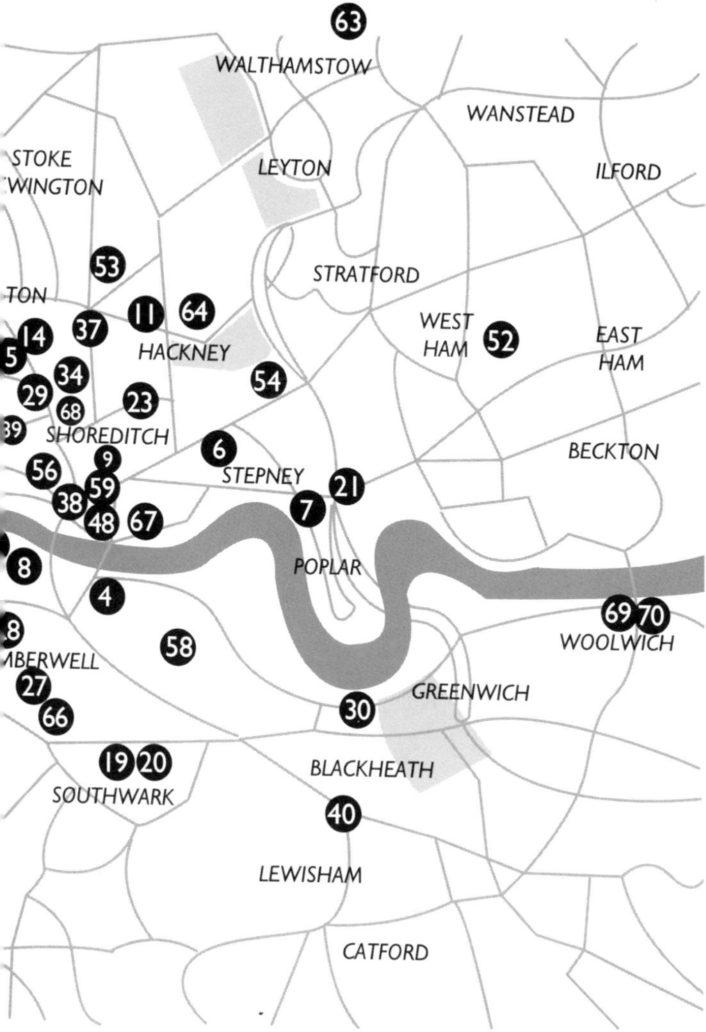

MAP

WALTHAMSTOW 63

WANSTEAD

STOKE
'WINGTON

LEYTON

ILFORD

53

TON

STRATFORD

37 11 64

WEST
HAM 52

EAST
HAM

5 14

34

HACKNEY

54

29

68

23

39

SHOREDITCH

BECKTON

56

9

6

STEPNEY

21

38 59

7

48 67

8

4

POPLAR

69 70

WOOLWICH

8

58

BERWELL

GREENWICH

27

30

66

19 20

BLACKHEATH

SOUTHWARK

40

LEWISHAM

CATFORD

3

BATTERSEA HIGH STREET, SW11

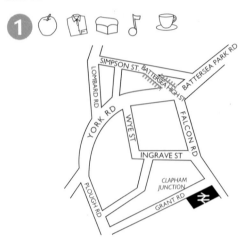

South end of Battersea High Street, up to the junction with Simpson Road.
BR: *Clapham Junction (Victoria, Waterloo)*
Buses: *239, 49, 319, 345*
Open: *Friday-Saturday 9.30am-4.30pm*

Backing into a scruffy residential area in the heart of what estate agents would probably call the "wrong" side of Battersea, this market certainly isn't the place to find SW11 trendies doing some picturesque pottering. First and foremost, Battersea High Street is doing what it's done for decades: supplying basic goods to local people – although the boarded-up shop fronts and slightly down-at-heel atmosphere suggest that trade has taken a turn for the worse in recent years.

Despite this, the street still has bags of character and some of the traditional shops should have design history enthusiasts grabbing for their cameras. Try Costa's Barbers for a timewarp haircut, or Jack Hall Dining Rooms for a sit down in what feels like the café time forgot – the menu is defiantly old school: Spotted Dick and Treacle Pudding are both just 70p a bowl. Notarianni & Sons ice-cream parlour is also a real one off, with a particularly impressive Deco-style

Battersea High Street

chrome-wrapped frontage (open for lunches on Mondays to Fridays only).

The market's short, double line of stalls pretty much sticks to the standards: fruit and veg (lots of good prices); a large card stall; pet food and accessories (with an extensive and grisly selection of pigs' extremities from 60p); biscuits, packet food and sweets; household goods; clothes (nothing special, but the odd thing is worth a look, e.g. a sturdy-looking fleece for £16), socks and underwear; and flowers. On first glance the tape and CD stall looks like a no-go zone full of fourth division retro horrors, but have a good hunt through and the odd bargain pops up in the compilation or cheap chart titles sections and albums start from only £1. The bread stall near the mouth of the market does tempting deals on bags of cakes, and the fresh ciabatta is good value at £1 for 3 small loaves. If you fancy getting your Sunday joint off the side of a lorry, then see what's on offer from the whole-sale meat van at the end of the street.

Getting a Stall

For further details contact Wandsworth Council (see appendix).

BAYSWATER ROAD & PICCADILLY, W2 & W1

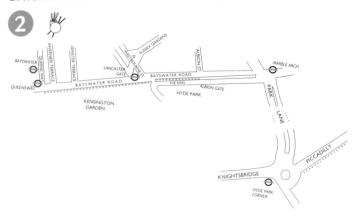

South side of Bayswater Road from Albion Gate to Queensway and south side of Piccadilly from Queen's Walk to Hyde Park Corner.
Tube: *Lancaster Gate, Marble Arch (Central), Green Park (Victoria, Piccadilly and Jubilee)*
Buses: *38, 22, 19, 14, 9, 8 (Piccadilly); 12, 94 (Bayswater Road)*
Open: *Sunday 9.30am-4pm*

On Sunday mornings hundreds of artists and art and crafts dealers set up stalls along Piccadilly and Bayswater Road. Although many of the traders sell their own work, none seem to be suffering for their art and a few appear to be thriving, parking their camper vans on the road and enjoying all mod cons while showing their work to the public. Things were not always this cushy as several of the longer-established traders recount tales of the sixties when the market was unregulated and traders often came to blows over pitches.

Green Park station is where the commercial-crafts goods are most heavily concentrated and includes the kind of trinkets found at most tourist markets: hippy/pagan jewellery, factory produced Egyptian artifacts and T-shirts with London buses and Beefeaters on them. Further west along Piccadilly you will encounter all sorts of art from reasonably tasteful watercolours to simply terrible oil paintings in large ornate gilt frames. With the very rare exception all the art work here is directly representational and concerns itself with a limited range of themes: rural landscapes, London scenes, still lifes and portraits of animals or pets. As I stood before yet another stall selling pictures made out of clock parts which also have a working clock in them, asking the all important question "who buys this stuff ?", an elderly American woman exclaimed "beautiful" and started bartering for the clock/picture of her dreams. Amid so many works of questionable quality, there are a few interesting stalls and Eileen Smith's watercolours were among the most accomplished and reasonably priced at between £65 and £100. I also liked the attention to detail in Jurek Jablowski's oil paintings of British pubs which were obviously popular judging by the newspaper clippings he displayed. Piccadilly Market ends at Hyde Park Corner and there is a ten minute walk through Hyde Park to Bayswater Road. If you need refreshment it's a good idea to get it now as there is nothing on Bayswater Road. Walk down White Horse Street (the north side of Piccadilly) to Shepherd's Market where there are lots of cafés and restaurants.

The Bayswater Road has some tacky craft stalls, but seems to be a little more art orientated and it is here that some of the best artists display their work. The large pop art canvasses were not bad value for £250. If you want a particular picture, Edwin Mendoza will do a copy of it for between £70-£300, the last time I visited he was close to finishing a copy of one of Modigliani's works. Among all the work on display one picture remains in my memory, it depicted a hawk about to get its claws into a very worried looking pigeon and was so comically bad it was rather good. Regardless of what you think of the art on display, Bayswater and Piccadilly Market is a great way to spend a couple hours on a Sunday and, with any luck, you might find the watercolour of Big Ben you've always wanted.

Getting a Stall

For further details contact Westminster City Council (see appendix).

BELL STREET, NW1

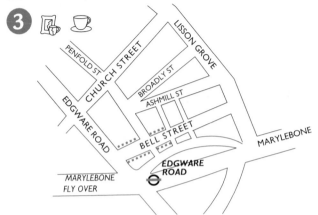

Western end of Bell Street, between Edgware Road and Lisson Grove.
Tube: *Edgware Road (District, Metropolitan and Bakerloo)*
Bus: *6, 7, 15, 16, 23, 36, 98*
Open: *Saturday 8am-4pm*

Bell Street is a great little junk market, and well worth a visit on your way to its much bigger sister market on Church Street (see page 58). Only about five stalls are set up on a Saturday but, amid the junk, there are always one or two surprises and quite a few bargains to be found. On a recent visit a man paid just £8 for a large Union Jack: he wasn't especially nationalist, he explained, but needed the flag for a play he was producing – a wonderful case of serendipity. A little further along I found a pair of cotton pyjamas for only 50p and a pair of roller blades in the right size for £7.

Jock has had a stall here for thirty years and enjoys talking about when the market was much larger, blaming its decline on the interference of Westminster Council. If the weather is bad or business slow, some stall holders pack-up early, so it's a good idea to get here before 2pm. The market has a few good places to eat and drink, among them The Green Man public house and La Belles snack bar. If you are a hi-fi buff then the two second-hand hi-fi shops on the street are worth visiting. The best way to get to Church Street Market is down Penfold Street, which also has a public garden half way down that's great if the weather is fine.

Getting a Stall

For further details contact Westminster City Council (see appendix).

Bell Street

BERMONDSEY, SE1

Bermondsey Square, between Abbey Street, Bermondsey Street and Tower Bridge Street.
Tube: *Borough, London Bridge (Northern)*
BR: *London Bridge*
Buses: *42, 78, 188 (Tower Bridge Street); 1, 78, 199 (Grange Road)*
Open: *Fridays 5am–12-1pm*

The whiff of a dodgy reputation still lingers around the capital's largest (and cheapest) antique market at Bermondsey Square – maybe it's the location, tucked south of the river in deepest SE1, or the fact that in winter the market kicks off in pre-dawn darkness, with dealers setting up from as early as 3.30am. Visitors hoping for a glimpse of illicit London will be disappointed, as Bermondsey Market is in fact the centre of a very serious antiques trade; the atmosphere in this attractive square is far more like a civilised continental flea market than a wide-boys' dealing den. That said, a lot of money changes hands as large numbers of focused buyers regularly come from abroad to pick up cheap items from the mass of antiques on show: displays encompass an almost overwhelming range of silver, jewellery, clocks, glass, prints, crockery and porcelain. A lot of well-informed scrutinising goes on down every row of stalls, as people pick over thousands of collectables.

Prices reflect the quality of the goods, with few glaring bargains jumping out from the spread of beautiful and unusual pieces on offer. Although friendly, it's unlikely dealers will do you many favours, especially on more unique objects, but appealing items can still be picked up for under a tenner – on a recent visit, a classic sixties plastic tortoiseshell bracelet was £6, a bundle of good quality butter knives £2 and fifties cocktail-lifestyle glasses £1 each. Shopping around can also reduce prices significantly, so don't go for the first example of something you like – it may well be £5 cheaper on a nearby stall. The costume jewellery is particularly interesting, with a lot of out of the ordinary pieces, for example, twenties vulcanite (a coal-based plastic) chain-link necklaces were going for around £35. It's refreshing that despite being a market full

Bermondsey

of generic antiques, outcrops of genuine idiosyncrasy are every-where at Bermondsey, with voodoo dolls lined up amongst Toby Jugs, and fifties iron 'n' spit-out tie presses ("See a tie fly!") next to Royal Doulton tea services.

The antiques trade also bleeds out into the streets around Bermondsey Square with large, warren-like warehouses on Long Lane, Bermondsey Street and the north section of Tower Bridge Street chaotically full of furniture and larger pieces of household kit. Prices won't impress the seasoned junk-buyer and the emphasis seems to be on fairly heavy, dark wood pieces but, if you persevere, you can probably find something interesting and of good quality for a reasonable price – Oola Boola on Tower Bridge Street stocks attractive twentieth-century items, like an Art Deco chest of drawers for £295. If after a few hours pottering you can bear yet more antiques, The Indoor Market on Long Lane has some quirky specialisms, with the clothes unit next to the entrance (nearest the corner of Long Lane and Bermondsey Street) stocking theatrically glamourous retro clothes and material.

Food provision in the immediate area of the market is pretty functional, but you can get a solid breakfast for well under a fiver at the trader's favourite, Rose's Café on Bermondsey Street, or in the Indoor Market's coffee shop (on Long Lane); alternatively, fill up alfresco at one of the market square's food stalls. Further away, Manze on the south end of Tower Bridge Street offers an authentic pie, mash 'n' liquor experience – for around £2 you can eat-in on scrubbed benches wreathed by steam from the eel pans simmering in the window. After breakfast, as the streets begin to thread with cars, get a real sense of the increasingly hybrid nature of the area by taking a walk up to the Delfina Trust Studios at the north end of Bermondsey Street which houses a contemporary art gallery as well as a restaurant that serves great coffee.

Getting a Stall
For further details contact Southwark Council (see appendix).

BERWICK STREET & RUPERT STREET, W1

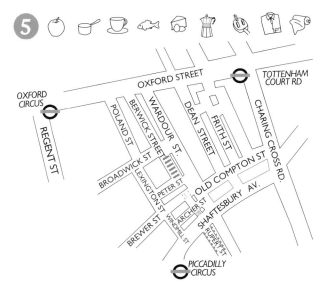

Berwick Street, from Broadwick Street extending south onto Rupert Street.
Tube: *Oxford Circus (Victoria, Central), Piccadilly Circus (Bakerloo, Piccadilly), Tottenham Court Road (Northern)*
Buses: *38, 19, 14 (Shaftesbury Avenue)*
Open: *Monday-Saturday 9am-5pm*

Berwick Street is one of those special places that seem to capture something of the flavour of London and its people. There's been a fruit and veg market here since the 1840's and although there are some signs of modernity such as the supermarket and tower block at the junction with Peter Street, the street and market still exudes much of its old character.

Berwick Street market is a one-off because it is essentially a local market dealing in fruit and veg, but situated bang in the heart of London's Soho. Despite being restricted to the west side of the street

13

and a cut in the number of stalls, Berwick Street is still a wonderful fruit and veg market with just about every fruit, vegetable and herb you could possibly need from the humble potato to Chinese black mushrooms and cassava. If you're looking for a particular delicacy the traders are always willing to point you to the right stall. More basic fruit and veg is often sold very cheaply with large bags of bananas, oranges or mushrooms going for £1, although it is a good idea to check the quality of the produce before buying. Supplementing the fruit and veg stalls are the long-established and excellent fish and cheese traders, as well as welcome recent additions like the fresh herbs and spices stall and the pitch selling all kinds of quality bread and patisserie. Berwick Street has several worthwhile shops as well, among them Simply Sausages, a good butchers, and many excellent fabric shops.

By walking south across Peter Street and through the narrow pedestrian Walker's Court (with porno outlets on either side), Rupert Street market can be reached. There are a few fruit and veg stalls here, but the main business is in clothing (new and second-hand street gear, as well as vintage), CD's and small electrical goods. The CD stall is part of Cheapo Cheapo Records (53 Rupert Street) which is one of London's best discount music shops and well worth a visit.

Anyone who loves London's markets must harbour some resentment towards Westminster Council for the changes in recent years, but the development of inner city supermarkets has also taken its toll on the market. On the positive side the number and variety of eating places on Berwick Street has greatly increased in recent years. Bar Du Marché and The Mediterranean Café are recent arrivals to the north end of Berwick Street, as is the trendy Beetroot cafe. Another welcome arrival is Tele Panino Italian café on Winnett Street (just off Rupert Street). For those wanting a pint in a traditional dingy British pub the King of Corsica back on Berwick Street will not disappoint.

Getting a Stall

For further details about a stall at either Berwick or Rupert Street contact Westminster City Council (see appendix).

Berwick Street

BETHNAL GREEN ROAD, E2

South side of Bethnal Green Road from Vallance Road to Wilmot Street.
Tube: *Bethnal Green (Central Line)*
Buses: *8 (Bethnal Green Road); 106, 253 (Cambridge Heath Road)*
Open: *Monday-Saturday 8.30am-5pm, Thursday 8.30am-12.30pm*

Flanking one of the East End's main thoroughfares, Bethnal Green
Road market is very much at the heart of the local cockney
community, famous for its humour and street-savvy banter. A walk
through the market should convince you this reputation is still well
deserved: no Pearly Kings, but plenty of rough diamonds of all ages
exchanging snatches of wit and good old-fashioned cheek –
customers and traders alike seem to love a chat, and some stalls
(especially ones selling fruit, veg and provisions) have lots of regulars.

As a fairly large, well-established market with a solid base of
local customers and a string of competing traders, Bethnal Green
Road can offer a wide range of goods at persuasive prices.
Everything you might need, from bedding to plugs, is available and
generally of reliable quality. There is nothing particularly out of the
ordinary here, but if you're after a relaxed, no frills market then this
one should fit the bill.

The fruit and vegetables are cheap (2lbs Katy Apples for 50p) and look fresh, the fairly conventional general selection supplemented by a single Afro-Caribbean stall. A few of the street's shops also sell food from period piece premises, evidence that there is enduring support for specialist trade in an area which seems to have avoided the total destruction of its retail traditions by the convenience revolution. The market's meat, fish and seafood stalls supplement some excellent butcher's shops, which offer impressive bargains on large joints and multi-packs of eggs (£1.69 for 30) – the old ladies know a good price when they see one, so follow their lead.

Bethnal Green scores high on the sartorial scale, with a spectrum of new men's and women's clothes ranging from middle-aged and functional to semi-designer jeans and jackets. Prices are often, to quote one trader's sign, "Bloody Cheap!", and there are indeed plenty of solid bargains on standard items like sweat tops, leggings and T-shirts. The underwear stalls are particularly good, with M&S remainders going for around half price, and plenty of nice cotton bras for £3. A number of rummage-style stalls also have super cheap separates or a lucky dip mixture of things like lipsticks, suntan lotion and hair products. The luggage and bags sold on the market are also slightly better looking than the drably functional clobber you get elsewhere.

Bethnal Green Road is well served by snack bars and cafés but two eateries are worth a special mention: G.Kelly serves pie and mash (£1.75) in a textbook marble and benches interior, while E.Pellici does Italian-cum-greasy spoon breakfasts and lunches. The latter has "local institution" written all over it: on site since 1900, this tiny café has beautiful Art Deco woodwork, yellowing celebrity pictures, genuinely charming staff, good quality comfort food (a delicious scone and tea is 90p) and bags of collective charisma.

Getting a Stall

For further details contact Tower Hamlets Central Market Office (see appendix).

BILLINGSGATE, E14

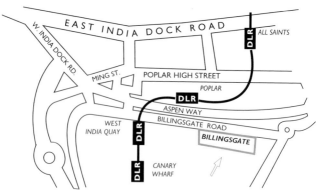

North quay of West India Dock, Isle of Dogs
Docklands Light Railway: *West India Quay*
Buses: *D1, D5, D8, P14, 277*
Open: *Tuesday-Saturday 5am-8.30am*

Billingsgate fish market was relocated to this modern warehouse in January 1982 from its old City location in Lower Thames Street from where it had been trading for nearly a thousand years. Billingsgate's new location has none of the atmosphere of the old building (which was designed by Sir Horace Jones) but, given the commercial nature of the market and the level of traffic in the City, such a pragmatic move was inevitable. The new market, although ugly from the outside, still has a great atmosphere and continues the great tradition of London's fish trade.

A stone's throw away from Canary Wharf, the market is easy to find – one dead giveaway are the seagulls which constantly circle above it, some of whom seem to have grown huge on the fishy titbits so readily in supply here. The place is busiest between 6.30am and 8am when most of the commercial buyers are doing business –

haggling over prices and checking the quality of the stock. Some of the traders are wholesale only, but it's worth asking first as many will do business with individual customers and newcomers are always given a friendly welcome. It's a great place to come with a recipe in mind and hunt down the freshest ingredients possible – the only thing to watch out for are the forklift trucks operating at the entrance to the market. Among the fifty or so traders you can find every kind of fish imaginable, such as white sturgeon, spotted dogfish, smoked salmon and large catfish still wriggling around in their polystyrene boxes. There's also a comprehensive selection of crustaceans and molluscs with anything from deep-water shrimps to live lobsters with their pincers bound to prevent an unwelcome nip.

If you're feeling hungry there are two cafés on the premises but they cater largely for the porters and, although you will be made to feel welcome, you will have to tolerate the ever-present aroma of fish. The only alternative in the area is MacDonalds on the mini roundabout approaching the market.

Billingsgate

)ROUGH, SE1

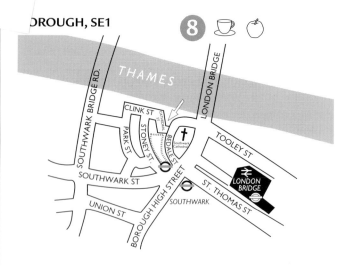

Main entrance on west side of Borough High Street.

Tube/ BR: *Southwark (Jubilee Line), London Bridge (Northern Line)*
Buses: *21, 35, 40, 133, P3, P11, D1, 344*
Open: *(wholesale) Monday-Saturday 3am-10am*
(Food Market) Friday 12noon-5pm, Saturday 9am-4pm, with a larger fair on the third Saturday of every month.

Borough is London's oldest wholesale fruit and veg market, with food having being sold on or near this site next to Southwark Cathedral since medieval times – it has been in its current home since 1756. Despite the area's historical pedigree there has (thankfully) been no attempt to flog the heritage angle at Borough and the market's unique character owes a lot to the fact that it is still purely a place people work, and work hard. Although one trader reported that business is being "slaughtered by the supermarkets", the pale early morning light still sees a steady flow of customers buying fresh essentials (for the grocery, market and catering trades) the low-tech way, from traders sitting in booths amongst huge piles of produce.

Only lost clubbers or the dangerously keen are going to stumble into the market during its peak business hours, but as the pace eases after 6am there's a good opportunity for the curious visitor to explore what is a fantastically atmospheric set of Victorian buildings. The whole place is perfect cinema-fodder. Crypt-like lock ups and ironwork arches hunker down in the vegetable-scented gloom under the angry rumble of trains crawling overhead. But beware too much gawping: traders are generally pretty tolerant but they are trying to work, so keep out of the way of the criss-crossing forklifts, barrows and reversing vans.

A trip to Borough is a powerful reminder of the sheer amount of food that London must get through in a day. Amassed fruit and veg begins to look strangely unfamiliar, as sprouts form towers of green sandbags, trays of apples and pears make huge nobbled carpets and battalions of spring onions lie to attention in rows of boxes. Not all the individual traders sell to the public, but if you lay on the charm somebody might let you have a bag of apples or pears.

Although the wholesale market is in decline there are defi-nite signs that this slice of SE1 is becoming newly vibrant as a place to stock up on quality food and drink: Neal's Yard Dairy (award-winning suppliers of cheese) have recently opened a unit on Park Street with a small retail section in front for the public; other busi-nesses establishing here include Konditor & Cook, de Gustibus and the very popular restaurant, fish! which has its own wet fish shop. As part of this regeneration a specialist food market has been running here every Friday and Saturday for the year and appears to be going from strength to strength. One stall sells over 20 types of mushroom and even has Spanish and French truffles (starting at £280 a kilo), as well as a variety of fresh herbs including chives, thyme and oregano. The prices are excellent with a good size bag of oyster mushrooms, a large bunch of rocket and several handfuls of fresh bay leaves coming to just £2. One of the largest stalls in the central part of the market is Sillfield Farm Products which sells fresh eggs, jams, all kinds of sausages (including wild boar), fresh meat and wonderful rich cheeses. As with many stalls here, there are lots of samples allowing you to try before you buy. Another trader offers New Forest cider and apple juice, and is keen to talk about his work. Having purchased a bottle of apple juice, he explained how a mix of Coxs and Bramleys gives just the right flavour. Other stalls include Furness Fish and Game which sells things like fresh pheasant and potted shrimps; Brindisa which specialises in Spanish food and has a great selection of olive oils; several excellent bakery stalls where the various loafs are still warm from the oven and a specialist producer of Dartmoor wild beef. The fresh fish stall seems good value with salmon steaks for £3.50 lb, and there is even a stall selling venison from the West Country. There are several fine cheeses stalls, another selling a selection of exotic bottled beer and a few smaller stalls with goodies like handmade chocolates and traditional puddings.

The Borough Food Market is proving a great success reversing the trend towards supermarket shopping. It's a wonderful place to witness the enthusiasm of the producers of fine food and those who want to buy it, many of whom are now regular customers here. Returning home with a bag full of fresh groceries I still had the taste of the delicious goats cheese I had sampled in my mouth and the memory of something even rarer – a British farmer smiling.

For food and drink during the wholesale market there are plenty of artery-lining eateries on Southwark Street and Borough High Street to cater for the breakfast faithful. Inside the market the traders' favorite, the Jubilee Café, where people take five over impressively cheap greasy classics. But if you don't fancy expletives with everything, opt instead for The Borough Café on Park Street. There are also a number of pubs which open under special license from 6am. During The Food Market Harpers Sandwich Bar on Southwark Street is a good place to find refreshment.

Getting a Stall
For a stall at the Food Market phone Anne Hastings 020 7 407 1800. Wholesalers should contact Guy Stanley 020 7 403 2238.

BRICK LANE, E1 & E2

Brick Lane (north of the railway bridge up to Bethnal Green Road), Bethnal Green Road (from Brick Lane to Commercial Street), Cheshire and Sclater Street.

Tube: Liverpool Street (Metro & Circle Lines), Aldgate East (District), Old Street (Northern), Shoreditch (East London Line)

Buses 8 (Bethnal Green Road); 67 (Commercial Street); 253, 25 (Whitechapel Road)

Open: Sunday 6am-1pm

With so many of London's markets ordered to conform with local government regulations Brick Lane is the last bastion of disorder and lawlessness and all the better for that. Brick Lane becomes the hub of a sprawling disorganised market every Sunday Morning. Below are the main parts of the market, but be warned that the market changes very regularly so keep your eyes peeled for new streets and archways that have given way to market fever.

Bethnal Green Road
(from Sclater Street to Commercial Street)

This narrow pavement is a favourite spot for many fly-pitchers who like to set out their grubby wares here. Several years ago the police started a crack down on this illegal activity, but the fly pitchers proved resilient and this part of the market is still vibrant. For a lot of people the chaotic squalor of the temporary pitches will be unappealing, but for the seasoned bargain hunter this is the first place to look for unusual treasures. Just about any kind of junk or bric-à-brac can turn up on these streets and in the lock-ups set into the railway arches. Among the main goods on offer are audio tapes, old bikes, cameras, clothes, electrical equipment and tools. Recent unusual things discovered here include a kitsch musical seventies lamp and a leather-bound German edition of one of Oswald Spengler's works. Little gems found among the junk such as these make this part of the market a great place to potter.

Sclater Street

The junction with Bethnal Green Road is where a regular bike stall sells cheap and cheerful new mountain bikes and there's also a stall selling healthy looking but not very exciting pot plants. Just to the left is the first of Sclater Street's courtyards, this one selling books and used office furniture. It is here that a sturdy clothes rail was found for only £15, a much better buy than the Ikea equivalent. Further along the street are stalls selling new goods including DIY tools and accessories, basic clothing, foodstuffs, and cheap trainers. The lock-ups to the right of the road are worth investigating, one sells pet goldfish (a remnant of the old Club Row market, now closed) and another stocks cheap cotton sheets, towels and overalls,

As you walk down Sclater Street the market opens up to the left to reveal an open square with many of the traders doing business from large trailers. It is here that you can see a few of the best sales people, using a microphone and an over-active imagination to generate business. The stall selling electrical goods has a good crowd as the pitcher asks them "who's wants a radio for a fiver, no sir put your money away I haven't finished yet, wait for it, wait for it..."

Brick Lane

I am a bit uneasy about buying anything from such stalls, but as a form of entertainment it's a genuine bargain. Among the better stalls in this part of the market is the one selling second-hand radios and hi-fi equipment like a Leak Receiver for £50. The second-hand bike stall is also interesting with prices starting from around £40 for a sturdy old upright gents bike. This part of the market has recently become the site for several shambolic junk stalls, an indication of the constant flux of Brick Lane. Another new addition to this area is the stall selling fine French cheeses, a welcome change from the glut of cheap food stalls.

At the far end of this courtyard is Bacon Street which connects with Brick Lane. This street used to be a quiet backwater where dodgy old geezers sold dodgy old goods, but is now a good deal busier with the opening of several new lock-ups selling books, bric-à-brac, furniture and some very cheap stainless steel pots. Just opposite the square, on the other side of Sclater Street, is another large courtyard selling tools, electrical goods, computer games, kitchen pans, bikes, and even fruit and veg. Although most of the goods are legitimate, you may find stolen goods here, most of which are easily identifiable. You don't have to be Sherlock Holmes to deduce that a top of the range mountain bike for only £300 is likely to be "hot".

Cheshire Street (from Brick Lane to Hare Marsh)

In the last six years Cheshire Street has undergone something of a transformation, with some of the old courtyards giving way to new housing and office space. This gradual process of development is not all bad for the market and there are signs that Cheshire Street is becoming gentrified, trendy even. In recent years a shop selling fashionable collectables has opened as well as a large retro furniture shop on the junction with Brick Lane and a few doors down there's a shop selling end-of-range fashionable street clothing heavily discounted. These new arrivals compliment the variety and disorder of the many stalls spread along Cheshire Street selling anything from colourful shirts to shoe laces, M&S trousers to Zimmer frames. Just on the corner of Grimsby Street is Blackman's

Shoe Shop, a Brick Lane institution which stocks cheap and sensible footwear. Further along there's a narrow alley where a few stalls selling interesting junk and second-hand DIY tools ply their trade.

Brick Lane
(from Bethnal Green Road to under the railway arches)

Ironically, Brick Lane is one of the quietest and least interesting parts of Brick Lane Market. The junction with Sclater and Cheshire Street is busy with passing traffic and the few fruit and veg stalls in this area are always buzzing with the stall holders hollering their wears. The north part of Brick Lane has fewer stalls but does have a good clothing stall selling high street seconds at knock down prices – trousers, shirts and jumpers for £10 each. The main attraction of this part of the market is the 24-hour beigel bakery which makes the freshest beigels in town.

South of the junction with Sclater and Cheshire Street, there are two large indoor markets under the arches. The one to the left on Grimsby Street sells bikes, furniture, records and bric-à-brac to peruse under its damp brick arches. Just outside the entrance a man selling kitchen equipment recently offered a large professional stainless steel cooker for £500, a good buy considering it would cost over £1,500 new. Just opposite Grimsby Street, the other cavernous indoor market sells second-hand furniture and bric-à-brac. Carrying on further south past Shoreditch tube station there are a few junk stalls which on fine days spread their furniture, bikes and books along Brick Lane. If you carry on further south you will encounter several new boutiques and trendy cafés which have recently sprung-up and are a sign of things to come and still further is the heart of London's Bangladeshi community with some of the best and cheapest Indian restaurants in town.

Getting a Stall

There are many privately run lock-ups at Brick Lane that will rent space on a Sunday, it's best to have a look around and choose your site. For all other street stalls contact Tower Hamlets Central Market Office (see appendix).

28

BRIXTON MARKET SW9

(a) Grenville Arcade
(b) Market Row
(c) Reliance Arcade
(d) Station Arcade

Brixton Station Road, Pope's Road, Atlantic Road,
Electric Road and Electric Avenue
Tube/BR: *Brixton (Victoria and Northern Line)*
Bus: *3, 109, 133, 159*
Open: *Monday-Saturday 8am-5.30pm, Wednesday 8am-1pm*

Brixton was a rather smart place in the last century and there are
still signs of its Edwardian grandeur in some of the architecture,
particularly along Electric Avenue (which was one of the first streets
to have electricity in the 1870's). The area was in decline for many
years but received a new lease of life when West Indians settled here
after the war. Brixton market is now the best weekday market south
of the river and a great place to visit if you're looking for fresh and
exotic food, Indian fabrics and there are even some good second-
hand stalls for those in search of bargains. The market is a sprawling
affair consisting of several roads, arcades and railway arches which
can be a bit disorientating, but there are good watering holes for
those who need to stop and get their bearings.

Electric Avenue

This is one of the main thoroughfares of the market and a great place to start if your interest is food shopping. There are lots of excellent fruit and veg stalls here, as well as a top-knotch fishmonger and butcher to complement the market. One of the most interesting stalls sells Afro-Caribbean spices, including something called edible chalk. There's also a very good Thai Supermarket near the junction with Atlantic Road, emphasising Brixton's cultural and culinary diversity. Food isn't the only thing on offer here and there are stalls selling cheap fabric, haberdashery, household goods, as well as one offering shoes for only £5 and one with watches going for the same price.

Pope's Road

This small road leads on from Electric Avenue, but has none of that street's charm. In place of Georgian architecture there are modern lock-ups lurking amid railway arches and an ugly Iceland supermarket. Making up for the environment are some very good fruit and veg stalls and quite a few stalls selling cheap fashion clothing and shoes, a kids clothing stall and one specialising in net curtains. One of the entrances for Granville Arcade is on Pope's Road, or alternatively you can continue on to Brixton Station Road.

Brixton Station Road

For those more interested in bargain hunting than food shopping this is the most rewarding part of the market. The Brixton Road end of the street is not that busy, but it does have a decent stall selling house plants and another selling cheap new clothes. Further along there are some good places to eat, among them Jacaranda Garden, the Max Snack Bar – which serves Portuguese food – and a kiosk serving Caribbean food. This part of the market only really gets interesting after the junction with Pope's Road, for it is along this stretch that all the second-hand stalls can be found. One stall specialising in used clothes had a YSL shirt for £3 and a French Connection men's jacket for only £4. A welcome addition to the market since the last edition of this book is Granny Hurlock's

Cavern which sells all kinds of junk with a particularly good selection of curtains and some very fine leather jackets. There are also quite a few electrical goods scattered about this part of the market and it was here that I found a cordless BT phone for only £12 and a JVC tape player for £30. If you fancy a high cholesterol treat after your endeavours, John's Café is at the far end of the market.

Granville Arcade

Although this is the largest arcade in Brixton Market it's surprisingly bright and airy with plenty of skylights and light-coloured walls. There are quite a few stalls stocking household goods, but this is a particularly good place to find exotic foods with many stalls selling Afro-Caribbean spices and flavourings, several good fishmongers and greengrocers as well as stalls specialising in Chinese and Asian ingredients. There's even a Chinese herbalist trading amid the food stalls for those interested in balancing their yin and yang. If you need refreshment there's an excellent Mexican Café within the arcade.

Market Row

This indoor passageway between Atlantic Road and Electric Lane is as pleasantly light as the Granville Arcade. It has some reasonable fruit and veg and street fashion stalls, but is clearly the best part of the market for cafés: with Kim's Café for basic grub, Café Pushkar for excellent veggie food and the very smart Eco Café for great pizzas and a mean cappuccino.

Reliance Arcade

This narrow passageway is darker than the other arcades in the market and has only a handful of stalls offering cheap shoes, clothes and CD's as well as a stall selling Jamaican patties.

Getting a Stall

For further details contact Brixton Market Office on 020 7926 2530 between 8.30am and 4.30pm.

BROADWAY, E8

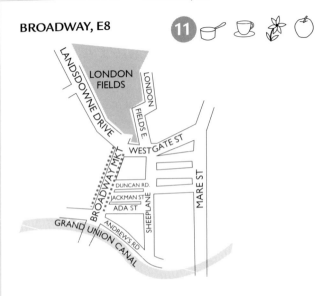

Broadway Market, between Westgate Street and Ada Road.
BR: *London Fields or Cambridge Heath (Liverpool Street)*
Buses: *(Westgate Street) 236*
(London Fields) 48, 55, 106, 236, 253, 277
Open: *Times were not yet established at the time of writing,*
phone 020 7249 2311 for further details.

Broadway Market is one of London's oldest markets – historically it was where farmers stocked up on provisions on their way back from delivering cattle to Smithfield Market (the herds themselves used to graze on London Fields before their final journey into the city). Sadly, what must have once been a thriving street community has now dwindled to only a few stalls selling fruit and veg, the decline starting with the demise of the GLC, former owner of Broadway Market's leases. Lack of money to invest in properties meant that the new owners, Hackney Council, had to raise rates, sparking a gradual desertion that turned the street into a gap-toothed strip of local shops punctuated by boarded-up shop fronts –

many still poignantly decorated with the names of businesses which were probably on site for generations.

Despite the radical shrinkage, Broadway Market doesn't feel like a place that's given up. This part of Hackney may look a bit shabby but the media set have spotted the potential in the area's elegant Georgian properties and already a number of specialist shops and initiatives reflect the recent change in the area's population. A hat shop, holistic health centre, Italian restaurant and the Hidden Art of Hackney project all sit happily amid the more traditional hardware stores, barbers, cafés and newsagents.

Local traders appear keen to capitalise on this general trend, having put together a regeneration package which aims to rebuild the market with a new focus on specialist stalls and shop units selling and making arts and crafts. Ann Cooke, Broadway Market enthusiast and proprietor of Cooke's pie and mash shop (an award-winning establishment of period elegance serving classic carbohydrates and veggie pies) is determined the street won't go any further downhill. The rescue plan includes putting a bar on the Regents Canal which runs along the bottom of the street and setting up pleasure barge trips to Limehouse Basin. Some of the new fashionable outlets opening on Broadway Market include an ultra trendy organic food and juice bar called Heroes of Nature, and Campus for hand made beds and futons.

Getting a Stall

For further details contact Broadway Market Traders Association on 020 7249 2311.

BROADWAY, SW17

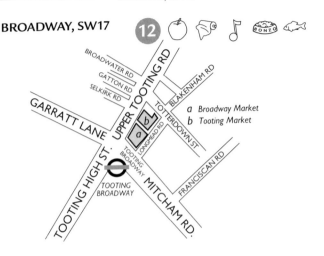

Upper Tooting Road.
Tube: *Tooting Broadway (Northern)*
Buses: *44, 77, 270, G1 (Garratt Lane);*
155, 219, 355, 127, 133, 264 (Upper Tooting Road)
Open: *Monday-Saturday 9.30am-5pm*
(til 6pm Friday and Saturday), Wednesday until 1pm

This covered market doesn't promise much from the street (the
entrance nearest the tube is a gap between tacky shops leading into
a dingy passage), but Broadway Market is certainly worth a look.
The lack of steady trade and a tendency towards half-hearted
presentation make it a bit underwhelming in terms of atmosphere,
but the mixture of standard utility fare and goods and services
aimed at local Afro-Caribbean and Asian communities means there
are plenty of cheap and interesting things to buy if you take time to
explore its main "square" and access passageways (two lead off
Upper Tooting Road).

Afro-Caribbean food and vegetables are well-stocked and supplemented by meat, sea food and fish stalls which all stick impressively
low prices on a wide range of stock, such as £9.99 for a big glis-
tening salmon. There is also an excellent fruit and veg stall at the

34

very back of the market, which has people queuing up enthusiastically for bargains like 2lbs of spinach for £1. The rest of the standard units offer lots of choice on household goods, stationery, underwear (including the exotic: £29.99 for an adult-sized nurse's uniform in lycra!), luggage and cosmetics, as well as the odd dollop of idiosyncrasy: the pasta-cum-artificial flower stall is a bit of a one-off. Fabric, haberdashery, Indian jewellery and accessories also get units to themselves so, for keen dressmakers, there's the possibility of knocking up endless ritzy outfits on the cheap. Other than the unit selling colourful kids' separates in the main square, the clothes on offer are pretty forgettable.

In amongst all this are specialist traders selling more unusual goods like African wood crafts, African batik and novelty balloons: order a while-you-wait balloon-twist giraffe for 50p. Broadway Market's nail salon can send you all Beverley Hills with glued on individual diamanté stars at 50p. The other unit worth a look is the fish and pet stall, which has tanks set up like an aquatic video wall, plus an impressive selection of kitschy fish accessories, plastic pond plants and general pet supplies.

Tooting Broadway is a bit of a café-free zone but the market's slightly dreary diner doesn't seem to be doing much to capitalise. It's probably best to fill up on something from the small Afro-Caribbean take-away (a plate of plantain and beans is £2.50) or go next door to Tooting Market which has a much more lively café. If you fancy a nibble while you shop, pay a visit to Who's A Poppin' which churns out doughnuts, candy floss and popcorn from inside a tiny unit near the market's second entrance.

Getting a Stall

For further details contact the market office on 020 8672 6613.

TOOTING, SW17

Upper Tooting Road.
Tube: *Tooting Broadway (Northern)*
Buses: *44, 77, 270, G1 (Garratt Lane);*
155, 219, 355, 127, 133, 264 (Upper Tooting Road)
Open: *Monday-Saturday 9.30am-5pm, Wednesday until 1pm*

A few yards further up Upper Tooting Road from Broadway Market is Tooting Market, its slightly smaller but livelier twin. Essentially this L-shaped covered market has the same sort of things on offer, with a range of utilitarian units dotted with the odd unexpected specialist. Again, meat, fruit and veg are well covered, but the fish stall at the market's left-hand exit looks particularly impressive with some very fancy varieties on display: baby sharks go for 99p a pound, and a huge bag of live mussels is just £2.50.

The Afro-Caribbean influence is strong, with a large grocery shop in the far corner selling endless varieties of exotic vegetables. The Vallo Oriental Shop makes the choice of food even more international with a shop unit crammed full of what looks like every imaginable noodle and cooking sauce, as well as a great selection of herbs, teas (good quality oolong and jasmine leaf tea are cheap) and unusual canned beans and vegetables at well below supermarket prices.

In amongst the remainder of the stalls (standard market clobber and a cluster of traders flogging naff reproduction furniture and paintings), there are a few other noteworthy units: The Trimming Centre does a massive selection of embellishments for clothes and furnishings, and a watch stall doubles up by selling a wide range of vivid Vietnamese satin dresses, shirts and slippers in both adult and child sizes (£40 for a full length Suzi Wong-style dress). If you want a sit down, The Grill and Sandwich Bar is a lively, unpretentious place for a cuppa or an ice-cream.

Getting a Stall
The stalls are all permanent. If you're interested ask for an application form from the tobacconist at the entrance to the market, from where the market is run.

CAMDEN, NW1

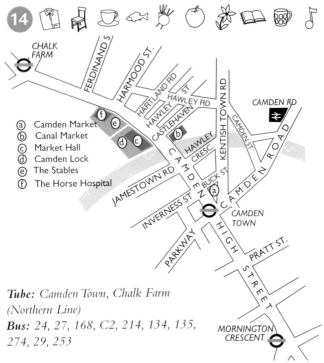

Tube: *Camden Town, Chalk Farm
(Northern Line)*
Bus: *24, 27, 168, C2, 214, 134, 135,
274, 29, 253*

Emerging from Camden tube station at the weekend, the visitor is
greeted with the beat of heavy bass music and the whiff of dodgy
burgers. Itinerant street traders stand around selling cheap lighters
and, unless you are here early, the streets will be packed with a largely
young crowd in search of fashion, music and much more. Camden is
a must-see for Europe's young and fashionable and, as one gangly
German youth exclaimed, it's "sehr Kool!". If you want a more sedate
market experience it's a good idea to visit here on a Thursday or
Friday when the southern part of the market is open and the atmosphere is a little more relaxed. Camden, like Portobello, is not a single
market but several markets in close proximity and complimenting
each other.

Camden Market
Camden High Street, south of Buck Street
Open: *Thursday-Sunday 9am-5pm*

This courtyard is the first part of the market encountered from Camden tube station and caters almost exclusively for the young and trendy (and those that aspire to be). Amid the narrow aisles crammed with stalls you can find some excellent new clothes, with a few independent designers selling their clothes at well below boutique prices. The funky women's designer jumpers found here recently were a snip at £15, as were the simple but well made grey cotton men's shirts for a tenner. There are also many stalls dealing in second-hand retro gear, with a few offering bargain rails and the occasional pile of jumble at even greater discounts. Although there is plenty of original and unusual clothing here, there are also lots of stalls selling basic street fashion at inflated prices and several dealing in the detritus of youth such as hippie tie-dye T-shirts, temporary tattoos and assorted cheap jewellery. With music stalls scattered about the market playing anything from reggae to current club sounds it is easy to get carried away and return home with some regretable purchase such as the packets of herbs which guarantee a "legal high".

If you don't like crowds try to visit this market on a Thursday or Friday when it's considerably quieter with a more relaxed atmosphere. On these days there are fewer stalls, and the traders are often a little cheaper and more prepared to barter. If you need refreshment after your search for street cred you could try the Chinese or Thai food stalls in the market or walk down Buck Street to the very trendy WKD café. There are also a cluster of good cafés on Inverness Street just opposite the market.

Getting a stall
On Thursday and Friday you should be able to get a stall by just turning up and speaking with Peter in his office at the back of the market. Stalls on a Saturday or Sunday are much more difficult to find and involve doing a stint on the less popular days and getting your name on a mysterious list (good luck).

Inverness Street Market
See entry on page 94.

Camden Canal Market

North east of the canal, and connecting with Castle Haven Road.
Open: *Saturday-Sunday 10am-6pm*

The narrow entrance to this market offers a range of novelty T-shirts, hippie gear and smoking devices that can be off-putting to the discerning but, once you get past this, the market does become more interesting. There are several excellent retro clothing stalls, a bookstall offering paperbacks for £1–£2, collectables and the occasional craft stall. A recent visit found a stall selling end-of-line fashionable trousers for only £7 and another offering well-made canvas shoulder bags for a mere £12. At the back of the market there is a stall offering used bicycles from £25. Although the market lacks a clear focus, its ramshackle nature gives it a charm of its own and there are some bargains to be found if you are prepared to hunt them out.

Getting a Stall

It is usually possible to get a stall by turning up by 8.30am and speaking to the market manager, but in the summer months it may be more difficult. Phone 020 7284 2692 for more details.

Camden Lock

North west of Camden Lock
Open: *Saturday-Sunday 10am-6pm, some of the shops and stalls are open during the week if you want to avoid the weekend crush.*
Friday 11am-3pm (Farmers Market)

It was the rapid success of Camden Lock market in the early seventies that transformed Camden and gave rise to all the other markets that now precede it on Camden High Street. In the last thirty years the site has undergone considerable renovation and development, but the original complex structure of buildings and courtyards remains and still looks good.

The canal with its lock lies to the left of Camden High Street as you walk up from the tube station and on fine days there are always people lounging around on the lock gates catching the sun. Just after the bridge stands the **Market Hall** which has two floors offering all kinds of arts and crafts from cheap colourful rugs for a tenner to large silver-framed mirrors for £150 as well as excellent modern glassware, stylish designer hats and a good book-

Camden Market

shop downstairs which is always worth a browse. The shops within this building largely deal in quality clothing and gifts and many of these are open during the week. The first floor gallery leads on to a further indoor market called **Dingwalls Gallery** which offers a mix of arts and crafts, second-hand books, collectables and second-hand clothing. It is here that you'll find Henry & Daughter which specialises in fine retro clothing.

Behind the Market Hall and accessible from the first floor back entrance or from the walkway running along the canal is a system of three interconnected open-air squares called the **East, Middle** and **West Yards**. This part of the market has a lot of souvenirs and novelty tat, but there are also many worthwhile stalls offering good value retro clothing, discounted new garments, funky clothes from independent designers, as well as the occasional book or music stall. At the far end of the West Yard is the Camden Bookshop which has a good stock and regularly discounts books and is also conveniently situated next to an open-air café which serves a tasty cappuccino. If it's raining try the HQ Café which is located on the first floor of the buildings surrounding the courtyard.

Further north lies a maze of archways, courtyards and passages crammed between the Market Hall and the Stables Market known as **Camden Lock Place**. The first passageway offers largely arts-and-crafts items of varying quality and several food stalls. It does, however, have a very well stocked little bookshop which is worth visiting.

Just a little further along with an entrance under the bridge is a large open yard with stalls and permanent archway shops largely catering for the youth market. There are several retro clothing shops with interesting stock and some discount rails and another stall offering quality men's shirts for only £8.99. To cater for the morbid (I only wear black) teenage crowd there is a gothic lock-up selling things like cups in the shape of a human skull for those who like to drink their tea on the wild side. If such nonsense is of little interest to you there are many food stalls with seating where you can gain sustenance before going on.

Getting a Stall
For further details about a stall at Camden Lock call 020 7284 2084.

42

The Stables Market
West of Chalk Farm Road.
Open: *Saturday-Sunday 9am-5pm*

Two narrow archways connect Camden Lock Passage with **The Stables Market** which begins with yet another courtyard made dark and slightly cramped by the two large buildings that stand within it. Here there are some of the largest lock-ups dealing in retro, cult and club clothing, some of which are situated on a raised platform only accessible by stairs. One of the largest shops in this part of the market is Cyberdog, which is a cavernous outfit selling street and club fashion and containing its own café. The smaller stalls at the far side of this yard are also worth a visit with lots of knick-knacks to rummage through and a stall specialising in second-hand camera equipment. There's also a good Thai food stall in this area, if you need refreshment before walking further.

The Stables Market has plenty of fashionable clothes and record stalls catering for the young, but also has a great range of shops and lock-ups dealing in antiques and collectables. Towards the far end of the yard is a huge building called The Horse Hospital which is where some of the best collectables can be found including books, picture frames and prints, watches, crockery and retro furniture. Most of the things here are not cheap, but they are of exceptional quality and rarity. If you are looking for a particular style of seventies sofa in a particular colour this is a good place to search.

If your budget is more limited and you like to rummage for bargains, the ascending path running along the side of The Horse Hospital is crammed with stalls selling clothes, and knick-knacks for a couple of quid an item. Although this part of the market is a little scruffy it is great fun and just the sort of place where with serendipity you can find something wonderful – it is here that I unearthed a Swiss ski jumper in perfect condition for just £3.

On the other side of The Horse Hospital at ground level are some of the smarter furniture dealers selling anything from fine antiques to art deco and modern design classics. This part of the market is a little quieter than the main square and with a Costa Coffee shop on the corner, is an excellent place to browse and relax after a hectic day in Camden.

Getting a Stall
For further details about a stall at The Stables phone 020 7485 5511.

CAMDEN PASSAGE, N1

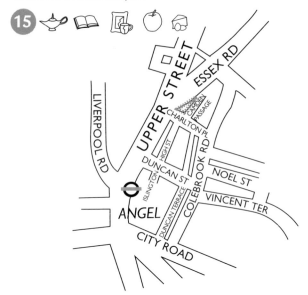

On the junction of Essex Road and Upper Street,
opposite Islington Green, N1
Tube: *Angel (Northern)*
Buses: *38, 56, 73, 341 (Essex Road) ; 4, 19, 30, 43, 38 (Upper Street)*
Open: *Wednesday 7am-2pm, Saturday 8am-4pm (Antiques)*
Thursdays 10am-4.30pm (Books), Sunday 10am-2pm (Farmers' Market)

Camden Passage market is not as old as it appears. Although many
of the surrounding buildings are centuries old and the market
specialises in antiques, the market actually started here in 1960 just
as Islington began to evolve into the salubrious neighbourhood it is
today. Ironically, Islington did have a long-established antiques
market north of Camden Passage, called Caledonian Market, which
moved to Bermondsey after the Second World War (see page 10).

The antiques and bric-à-brac market takes place on Wednesday and Saturday. Many of the stalls are at the north end of the passage, under a high roof which keeps out the worst of the weather. Here you can find some very fine antiques with hefty price tags, such as a silver serving spoon for the princely sum of £180. Among the more modest items for sale were an Omega wrist watch for £75 and a simple angle-poise lamp for only £10. Further south along the passage there is a regular stall selling beautiful antique wooden boxes for between £50 and £185. Also along here is the Camden Head public house which is a wonderful building (just look up and admire the rather ornate upper storeys so often missed when being jostled by the crowds). Outside the pub some traders sell junk from blankets on the pavement. Although a lot of the things on offer here are worthless, it is possible to unearth the odd charming knick-knack for a reasonable price.

Further south along the passage there's a small undercover market on the junction with Charlton Place. Here you can find an eclectic mix of silverware, paintings, china and cutlery such as the elegant silver-plated tea pot I discovered for just £8. Just opposite the stalls is Cloud Cuckoo Land, a small but interesting shop specialising in vintage clothing. Pierrepont Arcade has outside stalls and an indoor maze of small antique stalls selling anything from stamps to military medals. Within the arcade there's a small café where you can get a tea and listen to the local gossip.

On Thursdays, Camden Passage becomes the site of a small book market with traders setting up at the junction with Charlton Place and further along at Pierrepont Arcade. This is not the place to find expensive antiquarian tomes, but there is a good selection of paperback fiction as well as academic, travel, art, history and reference books. On a recent visit a hardback edition of Joyce's Ulysses was found for a mere £4 and a good condition paperback edition of Julian Barnes Metroland for £1.80. For those who prefer a bit of turgid romance there is always a heady mix of popular fiction by the likes of Catherine Cookson and Wilbur Smith. The book market is a little diminished during the harsh winter months, but still worth a visit.

Islington is awash with funky eating places and coffee bars, but one of the best and nearest to the market is Alfredo's at 4-6 Essex Road. If the market has not satisfied your need to shop, there's the excellent Past Caring junk shop about 2 minutes walk north along Essex Road.

On Sundays Camden Passage is the venue of one of the many farmers' markets being established around London (see pages 38, 40 and 164). Although this seems like a new idea, it's a throwback to the days when farmers brought their goods to market and sold directly to their customers. Around twenty stalls are set up here on a Sunday offering quality fruit and veg, homemade cakes, several stalls selling freshly baked breads and pastries and lots selling farm-made apple juice. Bearsted Vineyard sells its own range of British wines for Between £6 and £10 per bottle and Lane Farm has a stall selling sausages and other fresh meat. Other stalls worthy of mention include the one selling British farm cheeses and the West Middlesex Beekeepers who offer small jars of their honey for £1.60 and has the added attraction of a glass case of worker bees going about their business. The plant stall is not as cheap as Columbia Road Market, but has some nice plants and plenty of advice about how to care for them. One of the best things about this market is the contact you get with the food producers who's enthusiasm and commitment is infectious. A visitor to the Lane Farm stall sampled one of the sausages and ended up talking with the young man who had made them – an experience you don't get at Tescos.

Getting a Stall
Wednesday is the busiest day and the cost of a stall is £20. On Thursday and Saturday they're only £15. For further details contact Sara Lemkow on 020 7359 0190 or call into her shop at no.12 Camden Passage.
For further details about the farmers' market contact Nina Planck on 020 7354 9968

The Farmers' Market, Camden Passage

CHAPEL MARKET, N1

Between Liverpool Road and Penton Street N1.
Tube: *Angel (Northern)*
Buses: *30, 38, 43, 56, 73, 341, 419 (High Street);*
153, 274 (Tolpuddle Street); 30, 73, 214 (Pentonville Road)
Open: *Tuesday, Wednesday, Friday and Saturday 9am-5pm. Thursday and Sunday 9am-12.30pm.*

Islington has something of a split personality with some of the wealthiest people in London living cheek by jowl with some of the poorest. While Camden Passage antiques market (see page 44) caters for the former, Chapel Market definitely belongs to the latter camp.

Chapel Market began as, and continues to be, a local market in character, selling basic street fashion, fruit and veg, fresh fish, hardware, small electrical goods, cards and decorations, bags and shoes, pet food, spices and herbal teas. The market varies quite a bit in size with the greatest number of stalls at the weekend. Since the first edition of this book Chapel Market now has a stall catering for Afro-Caribbean shoppers with casava and yams as well as things like hot chilli sauces; it also has a new and very good charity shop near the junction with White Conduit Street where I recently unearthed a stylish leather jacket for £8. Just around the corner, on White Conduit Street itself, is a long-established junk shop known as the Old Furrier Shop because of the shop sign that still hangs above its door.

Hungry shoppers in search of a bite to eat and an escape from the hustle and bustle of the market are spoilt for choice. Look out for Aida's Café and the ever-popular baked potato stall in the market itself and Tony's Café on White Conduit Street. At the Panton Street end of the market there are a clutch of curry houses, Bel Poorhi being among the best, while Alpino's serves simple pasta dishes.

One of the best things about Chapel Market is that it co-exists with many High Street shops. There's a Woolies and M&S on the street and a Sainsbury's just around the corner. There are also several specialist food stores including Olga Stores, one of London's finest Italian deli's, on Penton Street.

Getting a Stall
For further details contact Islington Council (see appendix).

Chapel Market

CHARING CROSS COLLECTORS FAIR, WC2

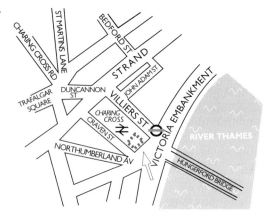

Under Charing Cross Arches at the southern end of
Northumberland Avenue
Tube: *Embankment (Northern, Bakerloo, District and Circle)*
Charing Cross/BR (Northern, Jubilee and Bakerloo)
Buses: *6, 9, 11, 13, 15, 23, 77A, 91, 176 (Strand);*
24, 29 (Charing Cross Road); 3, 12, 53, 88, 109 (Whitehall)
Open: *Saturday 8.30am-5pm*

Every Saturday, hundreds of collectors congregate in an unprepos-
sessing underground car park in central London. Among the fifty or
so stalls you can find military medals, coins, stamps, bank notes,
postcards, cigarette cards and even phone cards. Collecting things
seems to the uninitiated a dull and rather unexciting pastime and
the initial impression when entering this concrete bunker will
probably confirm this view. The average age of those attending is
about fifty, they are nearly all male and a very great number sport
beards of some description often in conjunction with a cardigan of
grey or brown hue. If you can resist the temptation to run, a brief
wander among the stalls is sure to unearth something of interest.
The coins on display are a good first stop because of their intrinsic
appeal. The neatly written labels give details of the type and age of

the coin and the dealer is usually willing to expound at length if you want to know more. I was surprised that some coins of considerable antiquity were so cheap. An English Half Groat dating from 1461 could be bought here for £16, a Roman Denarius for £23 and a Syrian coin from 142 BC for only £12. Other coins of various denominations and ages were piled in great heaps for only a few pence each. It is here that I discovered that my only family heirloom (a 1965 coin in commemoration of Winston Churchill) was worth the princely sum of 60p.

There are many stamp dealers here selling all kinds of stamps. It is possible to start a collection for only a few pence but in some instances whole collections are for sale. I asked one bearded, cardigan-clad stall holder the value of his most expensive stamp, but my question was clearly a crass one for his brow creased and he explained that he didn't think about his collection in that way and then generously volunteered the figure of £75 to help me.

The postcard stalls are a little more accessible to the first-time visitor. They are usually arranged by country or area, but in some cases by subject and are fascinating not only for the aging pictures on the front but often for the hand written messages to be found on the back, addressed to long deceased correspondents. The political postcards are interesting, one card commemorated the Locarno Conference of 1925 with pictures of the participants including a young Mussolini, while another French postcard used a cartoon to lambaste Prussian Imperialism. Although not a collector I was tempted by the notion of owning a little bit of history for only a few pounds.

I meandered through the rest of the fair unmoved by the large collection of phone cards and positively revolted by the idea of possessing war medals that had originally belonged to men who had paid a good deal more than a few pounds for them. I departed with only a large and shiny dollar coin to commemorate my visit and to add to my now much devalued heirloom.

Getting a Stall
For further details contact the market manager on 01483 281 771.

CHALTON STREET, NW1

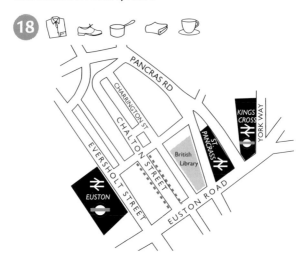

Chalton Street, between Euston Road and Churchway.
Tube: *Euston (Northern, Victoria), Kings Cross (Piccadilly, Metropolitan, Circle, Northern)*
Buses: *10, 18, 30, 73 (Euston Road)*
Open: *Friday 12-2pm*

Tucked away in an easy-to-miss location off the Euston Road, Chalton Street is a slightly anonymous market serving the predomi-nantly Indian and Pakistani community from the large public housing estates of Somers Town. The area's obviously had a rough time of it recently: the majority of shops are boarded up or empty, the market has been downsized to once-a-week opening and there are plenty of gaps in the pitch line up. Nonetheless the market is pretty full of people on a Friday lunch time, with streams of shop-pers clutching bags bulging with mass purchase loo rolls or cleaning fluids. Chalton Street may show the signs of decline but its market still plays a significant role in supplying cheap, utilitarian goods to local people without the luxury of consumer choice.

All markets offer some serious bargains on household goods, provisions, stationery and odds and ends of all kinds, but Chalton Street is a bit special. Put together, its stalls stock a massive selection of items, with plenty of persuasive prices: 3 flannels, or a big bunch of fake chrysanthemums or 3 bags of pistachio nuts for a £1; a large aluminium cooking pan for £3.99. Family-sized bags of things like kitchen roll and cloths are also really cheap. Inevitably, there is a lot of tat in the mix, but have a good pick through and you could easily equip your kitchen with all the necessaries at a serious reduction on shop prices.

The rest of the market is made up of a fairly standard combination of stalls, although fresh produce is limited to one stall stocking a range of ethnic fruit and veg (some good bargains on big bunches of mint, or bags of limes). There is a wide range of new clothes on offer, some fashionable options sprinkled amongst a fairly forgettable selection of men's and women's separates. Sportswear is better, with functional sweat tops and bottoms going for £4.99, and brand-name trainers at around £5 cheaper than the shops. But Chalton Street really scores on smaller items like socks (men's at 60p a pair), vests (£1.80) and children's clothes: the choice is huge, with large blocks of rummage boxes full of bibs, baby gro's, school jumpers etc at rock bottom prices (3 pairs of underpants for £1) attracting an eager scrum of local mums.

Material and haberdashery are also well represented here, with most fabrics going for around a £1 a metre – a few stalls of ritzy jewellery and accessories are also on hand to kit out glamour pusses. Bargains towels and bedding can be snapped up at the stall near the Euston Road entrance.

Despite the gap-toothed look of the street, there is still enough local trade to keep three snack bars going. The best by far is Linares, a charismatic Spanish take-away/diner which has been serving good quality cheap sandwiches and lunches (paella or vegetarian moussaka for around £3) since 1845.

Getting a Stall
For further details contact Camden Council (see appendix).

CHOUMERT ROAD, SE15

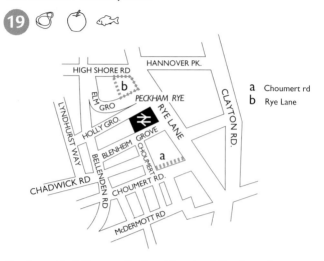

19

a   Choumert rd
b   Rye Lane

Rye Lane end of Choumert Road, and into Atwell Road opposite.
BR: *Peckham Rye (London Bridge)*
Buses: *12, 37, 63, 78, 312, P3, P12, P13 (Rye Lane)*
Open: *Monday-Saturday 9.30am-5pm*

One of London's Chartered Markets, Choumert Road has been the site of a provisions market for well over a hundred years; a variety of old signs, left like historical limescale on the little shops, are evidence of its long-standing position at the heart of Peckham's food district. Due to changes in the make-up of the local community and the resulting influx of international food shops into the area over the last quarter century, the goods at Choumert Road are now just one of many options amidst a bewildering tide of multi-cultural foodstuffs engulfing both Rye Lane and the roads which run off it. But despite massive competition – and the fact that, sadly, in this Peckham market you're not going to find local icon Del Boy flogging cordless teas-mades – the market looks as though it still has enough scruffy charisma to keep it alive for another hundred years. Fifteen or so stalls (pitched close to the row of specialist food shops to create a colourful corridor of produce) still attract a steady flow of customers with plenty of bargains and friendly banter. Times have changed so a lot more than just the humble spud or greens are on offer in the market, put together the range available is like a United Nations of fruit and veg: whether you're cooking Moroccan, Thai or Afro-Caribbean, one of Choumert Road's traders should be able to supply the ingredients.

Even if you're not buying, just walking through the stalls is a real foodie treat, with loads of unusual shapes and smells to savour. Local rivalry keeps the prices pretty cheap, five large juicy sweetcorn sell for £1 and a massive watermelon for £2.90. Across Rye Lane at the end of Atwell Street there is an additional fruit and veg stall which has the locals queuing up, so shop around.

Choumert Road is essentially a food market, but a few stalls at the Rye Lane end also sell standard items like underwear and luggage. The street's shops supplement the provisions on offer, selling predominantly African and Afro-Caribbean specialisms – Kubi's has beautiful batik and Jay Gee's music shop stocks every type of African Music – household supplies and toiletries, cosmetics, jewellery, shoes, fish and meat. Need something "sorted"? Stashed away at the end of the row of shops lurks Strictly Confidential, a "surveillance and investigation specialist" which has an unnervingly up front stock list painted on its windows, including phone taps, spy cameras and bullet-proof vests.

With food everywhere you look, Peckham is heaven for the peckish but if you prefer to eat sitting down, try the Choumert Café (next to Strictly Confidential) for no-frills English or Caribbean greasy spoon classics.

Getting a Stall

For further details contact Southwark Council (see Appendix)

RYE LANE, SE15

West side of Rye Lane, between Elm Grove and High Shore Road.
BR: *Peckham Rye*
Buses: *12, 37, 63, 78, 312, 345, P11, P12*
Open: Monday-Thursday 8.30am-5.30pm, Friday-Saturday 8.30am-6pm

Further north up the main road is Rye Lane Market, an indoor market which has been going since 1939. Although some traders are doing their best, the atmosphere is a bit low octane compared with the lively mixture on the high street. The market's main space has more empty units than occupied ones and many traders seem to be just making a quick buck on a single consignment of stock, so there are lots of half-empty shelves. Cottage industries and provisions shops aimed mainly at the Afro-Caribbean community are tucked away amongst the boarded-up units, along with a few other traders selling utility items like giant cooking pots, foam and electrical goods, as well as second-hand clothes.

But Rye Lane Market isn't totally underwhelming, having its fair share of well-presented shops selling a wide range of goods including toys, new clothes, bedding, meat, carpets, bags and luggage, underwear and general junk. Highlights are the fantastically well-stocked haberdashery unit, which does a great range of fun fur at £5.40 per metre; the perfume and toiletries shop opposite the end of the access passage from Rye Lane does good deals on name brands; and the mini garden centre has plenty of bargains for the green-fingered. Rye Lane Market is also the place to find, The Budgie – a pet homes and accessories unit which, from the looks of it, must have been supplying Peckham's tweeters since the market opened. If you're after a cuppa, Rye Lane Market only has Aunty's Café for on-site refreshments.

Getting a Stall
Rye Lane is being closed and redeveloped from April 2000 and no stalls will be available until later in the year.

CHRISP STREET, E14

Market Square, Chrisp Street
DLR: *All Saints (Fenchurch)*
Buses: *D8, D7, 309*
Open: *Monday-Saturday 9.30am-4pm*

This market has been in existence for over a century, pre-dating the rather ugly post-war architecture which now surrounds it. In 1994 the council built a futuristic new roof for the market from metal, concrete and glass, which helps keep the rain off and is about the most attractive structure in the area. Suspended from the roof are large posters showing the market in its Victorian heyday. The market now offers quality fruit and veg as well as lots of stalls with competitively-priced street fashion, sports wear and fashionable kids' clothes. The underwear stall is worth investigating with 3 pairs of cotton socks for only £2.50 and cotton T-shirts for a mere £1.99. When I last visited the market in the winter, several stalls were selling trendy fleece jackets for just £20. Other stalls offered videos, CD's, kids' buggies, haberdashery, Asian fabrics and good-value cut flowers. The market is complemented by the surrounding shops which include a good butcher and fishmonger and a local supermarket. For on-the-hoof refreshment there are several stalls selling basic British grub and The Curry Hut which serves up Indian food. The most popular eating places in the area are JP's Café right next to the market and Maureen's Cockney Food Bar which is situated a little further back.

Getting a Stall

For further details contact Tower Hamlets Central markets Office (see appendix)

CHURCH STREET, NW8 & W2

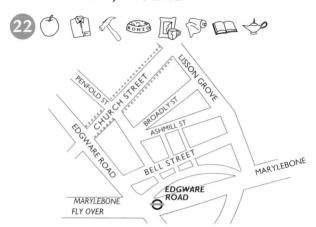

Church Street from Edgware Road to Lisson Grove.
Tube*: Edgware Road (District, Metropolitan and Bakerloo)*
Buses*: 6, 16, 18, 98 (Edgware Road); 139, 189 (Lisson Grove)*
Open*: Tuesday-Saturday 9am-5pm*

Church Street market has a relatively central location, but few
people outside the immediate area actually visit it and if they do it
is usually by accident in the process of visiting the famous Alfies
Antique Centre which lies at the Lisson Grove end of the street.
For this reason, Church Street Market has managed to maintain a
friendly community feel, with lots of the stall holders taking time
out to have a natter with one of their regular customers. This part
of the Edgware Road (just past the Marylebone fly-over) is pretty
down at heel and many of the stalls concentrate on the cheap and
cheerful rather than better quality goods. The £60 leather bags of
Leather Lane Market are not to be found here, but the two stalls
selling shoes for £5 a pair are always surrounded by eager bargain
hunters. Church Street is a good market to stock up on basic fresh
fruit and veg, but there is very little of the exotic on offer. Likewise,
the fresh fish stall is excellent for things like cod fillets and sprats,
but Red Snapper or squid are strangers here. Just opposite the fish

stall is one selling shellfish which cooks mussels and prawns with garlic and sells them hot and aromatic for £3 a packet. The stall is on the junction with Salisbury Street, but is easy to find if you just follow your nose. Nearby there's a stall selling dried fruit, nuts, pulses, beans, spices and herbs which is well worth a look.

Although many of the clothes on offer on Church Street are cheap and tacky, there are several stalls selling interesting stuff such as the one offering colourful designer shirts (probably copies) for £10 and the stall offering quality leather belts for between £6 and £10. Other items on offer include pet food and toys, household goods, children's clothes, fresh flowers, underwear, bedding and towels and even a stall selling vacuum cleaner parts.

At the junction with Salisbury Street, Church Street undergoes a subtle transformation as modern buildings give way to well preserved 19th century shop fronts, many of them dealing in fine antiques. It is at this part of the market that you'll find Alfies Antiques Market with four floors of antiques and a roof-top café. Outside the building a few stalls set up on a Saturday selling knick-knacks and jewellery. This part of the market would benefit from a few junk stalls to compliment the many antique shops, but the market changes little despite the change in surroundings. The best thing about this part of the market is the excellent fabric stall selling basic material for as little as 50p a metre. On Saturdays Bell Street Market is five minutes walk south along Penfold Street, and should not be missed by bargain hunters (see page 8).

Church Street has no smart restaurants but is awash with simple eating places. Among the most popular on Church Street are the falafel stall (reflecting the large middle-eastern community in the area), the Market Grill which serves both English and Thai food and the Surprise Café near Lisson Grove. On Edgware Road there's always the Regent Snack Bar which still has its original 1930's formica interior. If you want a pint look out for The Traders Inn or The Duke of York, both on Church Street.

Getting a Stall

For further details contact Westminster City Council (see appendix).

COLUMBIA ROAD, E2

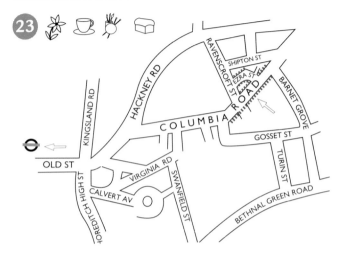

Columbia Road east of Ravenscroft Street to Barnet Grove
Tube: *Old Street (Northern), Bethnal Green (Central)*
Buses: *26, 48, 55 (Hackney Road); 8 (Bethnal Green Road)*
Open: *Sunday 8am-1pm*

Columbia Road Market is a Mecca for the green fingered with the
best selection of bedding plants, potted plants, bulbs, seeds, cut flowers
and garden pots to be found in the capital. It's a good idea to
approach the market from the west, so you can work your way
towards the best coffee shops which lie at the eastern end of the
street. Whatever direction you approach the market it is easy to find
by simply walking in the opposite direction to those weighted down
by trays of bedding plants, cut flowers or a large palm.

As you approach Ravenscroft Street there are several gift shops
catering for the smart crowd that visit here every Sunday. Among the
best shops in this part of the market are Pot Luck which sells simple
and cheap white crockery and The Pot Centre which offers a great
range terracotta pots at very competitive prices – a large terracotta
pot measuring 8 inches in diameter costs only £1.99. It's a good idea

to wait until the end of your visit before buying these bulky bargains – thus avoiding the inconvenience of lugging them around for the duration of your visit.

The market proper begins at the junction with Ravenscroft Street where stalls are crammed along both sides of the road. The stalls selling cut flowers are always busy, offering bargains like Dutch irises for £2 a bunch, twenty English roses for only £4 and tulips for a mere £1.50 a bunch. My last visit was in the winter and the market was without the trays of bedding plants which are so popular with the punters in the spring and summer months. Even on a winter's day there is plenty here to attract the eye with greenery like lemon-scented goldcrest for £4 a plant (3 plants for £10) and large eucalyptus plants for only £1.50. While the nursery-grown plants offer instant greenery, the stalls specialising in bulbs are doing good business with those gardeners that are planning ahead for the next season. There are also some huge plants to be found here at well below nursery prices, such as six-foot–high palms for £15 and orange trees (bearing small fruit) for £20 – the latter being reduced to £15 as the market neared its close. It is these huge plants that you often discern making slow and shuddering progress above the crowds obscuring the person carrying them and reminding the observer of a well-behaved triffid.

Columbia Road

Besides the plants there are several other attractions in this central section of the market. Idonia Van Der Bijl is an excellent and long-established gift shop and just a few doors down is The Columbia Pottery which is a fruitful source of pots for your new flora. Just opposite is Juno's – another busy gift shop. If you're feeling peckish already, and don't mind eating on the move, Lee's Sea Food sells fried calimari and giant prawns with a wedge of lemon and is highly recommended. Café Columbia is also a good place to stop if you want to sit down and catch your breath.

The junction with Ezra Street is where the flower stalls give way to some interesting shops such as Marcos and Trump for gifts and several antique and collectables shops. The Laxeiro Tapas Bar and further along The Globe Organic Café are both safe bets for refreshment. It is at this junction that some very good value shrubs and herbs can be found and the stall selling cut flowers is probably the best in the market – although also the most expensive. The market does not stop here as there are several flower stalls and several popular gift shops in the narrow courtyard just off Ezra Street and further along there are a series of large courtyards selling ornaments and pots for the garden, the largest being S & B Evans & Son. At this point the market finally ends leaving you with nothing to do but visit the courtyard behind The Royal Oak for a coffee and pastry or stop off at the excellent coffee shop located in the alleyway. If you fancy getting some fine food to take home with you try S. Jones provisions.

Columbia Road is a fun way to spend a Sunday morning even for non gardeners but, if you do choose to spend some money here, it's advisable to go armed with some idea as to what effect you want to create in your little Eden and avoid the impulse buy which is so easy when the plants look good and the prices are cheap. If Columbia Road has not exhausted your hunger for bargains, don't forget that Brick Lane and Spitalfields Market are within walking distance.

Getting a Stall

For further details contact the Tower Hamlets Central Markets Office (see appendix).

IDONIA VAN DER BIJL

Established in 1979, Idonia specialises in hand-made and designed products from home and abroad. Extensive travelling results in an unusual annual collection of artefacts, bought directly from the makers. The shop also specialises in quality glass and products relevant to the flower market.

122, COLUMBIA ROAD, LONDON E2 7RG
OPEN SUNDAYS 9AM-2.30PM
TEL: 020 7729 7976

THE COURTYARD, WC2

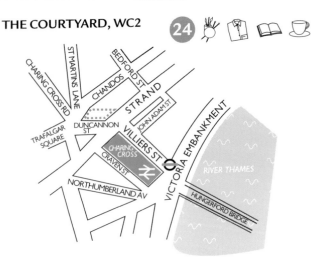

St Martin-in-the Fields Church Courtyard, off Trafalgar Square, WC2
Tube/BR: *Charing Cross*
Buses: *6, 9, 11, 13, 15, 23, 77A, 91, 176 (Strand);*
24, 29 (Charing Cross Road)
Open: *Monday-Saturday 11am-5pm, Sunday 12noon- 5pm*

There's been a church on this central London site for nearly a
thousand years – although the present edifice is the work of James
Gibbs and dates from 1724. The market is a much more recent
development, having been set up in the early 1980's, and largely
caters for tourists. The Trafalgar Square end of the market is awash
with Union Jacks, T-shirts with pictures of red buses on them and
Beefeater dolls and is best avoided. Further into the market many
nationalities are represented, there are jumpers from Peru, ornaments of Hindu deities, Egyptian-style paintings and models of
pharoahs (some dating as far back as 1993), African masks and silk
dresses from China. It is inexplicable why a market in the centre of
London and catering largely for tourists should sell so many
souvenirs of other countries – do visting French tourists return
home with a realistic plastic model of Tutankhamun saying "look

what I've brought back from London!" For that matter, do you find models of the Tower of London in Paris markets?

It is both easy and enjoyable to criticise this market, but among the thirty or so stalls I did manage to find one or two interesting things such as the men's Moto jacket for £29.95 and canvas body warmers for a reasonable £18.99. The book stall has a small but good quality mix of mint condition literature for about half the retail price. During the summer the market is a lot more vibrant and a few food stalls appear on the scene. The church hosts lunchtime music recitals and in-house refreshments can be found in the Crypt Café (entrance on Duncannon Street) in the church's basement.

Getting Stall
For further details contact Arthur on 020 7930 7821.

Covent Garden

COVENT GARDEN, W2

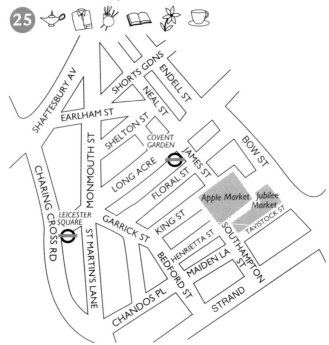

Covent Garden Piazza

Tube: *Covent Garden (Piccadilly)*

Buses: *6, 9, 11, 13, 15, 23, 77A, 91, 176 (Strand)*
14, 19, 24, 29, 38 (Charing Cross Road)

Open: *Monday 9am-4pm (Antiques), Tuesday-Sunday 9am-4pm (Arts, Crafts and Souvenirs)*

With its trendy shops and alfresco cafés, Covent Garden is one of the most popular shopping destinations in London and the main market area is usually brimming with visitors, particularly in the summer. This is a surprisingly recent phenomenon – until 1973 the grand architecture of the piazza housed the largest fruit, veg and flower market in the city. The whole of this commercial operation relocated to Nine Elms, Battersea (see page 43) and in 1980 Covent Garden reopened as the capital's biggest craft market. However, since the last edition of this guide in 1994, one of the few areas dedicatd to market traders has been closed to make way for the recently-refurbished Royal Opera House, leaving just two independant markets which together make up Covent Garden Market.

Apple Market

The Apple Market occupies the west corner of the piazza, designed around 1830 by Charles Fowler, and now has many smart shops housed within its structure. On Mondays the market is given over to antiques, with many of the same stall holders that do business at Portobello and Camden Passage Market resurfacing here. This is a good time to visit the market and there are lots of genuine antiques for your inspection.

For the rest of the week the market concentrates on arts and crafts with wares ranging from sterling silver jewellery, painted flower pots and quality children's clothes to more tacky souvenirs. Although some of the items stray beyond the bounds of good taste its good fun shopping here, particularly when the weather is fine and the buskers are in full swing. On a recent visit an entire orchestra was playing in the square, their rendition of Holst's *Mars suite* providing a dramatic accompaniment to my inspection of plastic novelty pigs and illustrated toilet seats.

Getting a Stall

For further details about getting a stall here during the Monday antiques market phone 020 7240 7405. If you would like more information about the Apple Market between Tuesday and Sunday phone 020 7836 2139.

Jubilee Hall Market

Jubilee Hall is a large wrought iron structure and, unlike the Piazza, it is given over entirely to market stalls, although it is often missed by the less determined shopper as it is set further back from the main thoroughfare . On Mondays Jubilee Market, like the Apple

Covent Garden

Market, concentrates on antiques but during the rest of the week it becomes a more general market catering largely for younger people. The stalls selling street fashion are reasonable value with quite a few discount rails offering garments for £5. There's also an army surplus stall which is popular with the teenagers who, although often disliking the army, are very keen on the clothing. The poster stall also aims squarely at the teenage punter with the ubiquitous Spice Girls and Leonardo di Caprio posters on display. There are clothes here for smarter middle-aged women too but, with the closure of the Opera House Market (which catered largely for the young), it seems that the Jubilee Market has filled the vacuum for teen wear. At the weekend the Market becomes more craft orientated but the change is slight and there should still be enough here to attract the passing teenage tourists.

Getting a Stall

For further details about getting a stall at the Jubilee Market phone 020 7836 2139.

EARLHAM STREET, WC2

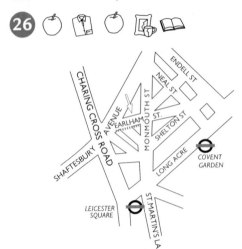

Earlham Street, between Shaftesbury Avenue and Seven Dials.
Tube: *Leicester Square (Northern and Piccadilly),*
Covent Garden (Piccadilly)
Buses: *14, 19, 24, 29, 38, 176*
Open: *Monday-Saturday 9am-5pm*

This street used to be the site of a thriving community market, but
the local immigrant community left long ago and the market now
caters for tourists and those who work in the area. The last fruit and
veg stall closed in 1995 and the market now trades in second-hand
and new clothing, modern jewellery and CD's with an excellent
flower stall situated on Seven Dials. The new clothing stalls are the
best thing about this market, with the two regular stalls stocking
well-made fashionable tops, trousers and skirts at competitive prices.
The women's zip-up hooded woollen tops for £15 were very good
value, as were the baggy canvas trousers for £25. There are usually
several interesting second-hand/vintage clothes stalls, but these are
less regular in attendance. One of the best changes to the street in

Earlham Street

recent years has been the arrival of a smart Oxfam Origin shop selling the best clothes donated to Oxfam from hand-made shirts to classic leather jackets. Another new arrival, the Juice Bar, is a good place to get a drink and inspect your new purchases. If its too busy, as it often is, try the Monmouth Coffee House, just around the corner.

Getting a Stall

For further details contact Camden Council (see appendix).

71

EAST STREET, SE17

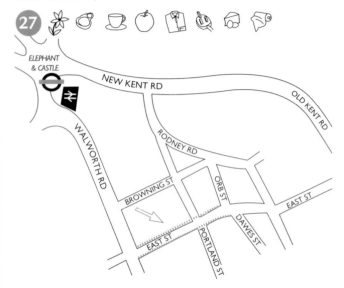

East Street between Walworth Road and Dawes Street.
Tube: *Elephant & Castle (Northern, Bakerloo)*
Buses: *12, 35, 40, 45, 68, 171, 176, 468, X68 (Walworth Road);*
P3, 42 (Thurlow Road)
Open: *Tuesday-Sunday 8.30am-4pm (busiest at weekends, when the street's shops are open both days).*

The birthplace of Charlie Chaplin, East Street is also home to one of South London's biggest, busiest and loudest markets. At weekends, with stalls squeezed between shops along the length of the long street, it begins to look like Oxford Street in miniature – tides of determined shoppers weave around clumps of slow-moving bargain hunters as the queues build for cut-price essentials. Inserted amongst some of the area's largest housing estates, East Street has a long history of serving the practical needs of local people, so craft fair trinkets are nowhere to be seen on stalls crammed with everything useful, wearable or edible.

East Street

Unlike a lot of other markets, in East Street you can still find a genuine sense of community, with dollops of classic South London humour, a real mix of shoppers, plenty of banter and noisily competitive traders stoking the lively atmosphere. The market isn't a wise choice for the delicate or the hung over; as one lady sighed recently as she entered the Saturday scrum at the Walworth Road junction: "...this place is no good for my nerves." On busy days you will need to watch out for serious jostlers, and East Street can also bring new meaning to the phrase "price wars" as you get caught in the crossfire between sellers as "Oi! Come on, who wants a bargain?", "Two pounds of mush' a nicker" punch repeatedly into the air above your head. But the demonstrations of iron-larynxed stamina and word-mangling delivery make brilliant free entertainment.

The size of the market means that lots of rival traders have to compete on price, so make sure you don't part with your cash without first checking out the opposition (also be aware that stalls change position or are absent altogether depending on the day, so your bargain may have disappeared on a repeat visit). East Street offers all the staples characteristic of any large street market, with lots of great bargains for the discerning shopper amongst piles of household and electrical goods, CD's, bedding and carpets, sweets, luggage, perfume, toiletries, jewellery, toys, fruit and veg (some Caribbean as well as standard English), wholesale meat, plants and flowers, with a few specialisms like herbs, spices and cheese also going cheap.

Certain things do stand out. East Street is full of clothes, and many of the shops and stalls offer impressive reductions on chain store prices – underwear, dresses, and shirts are often good value – although sifting is essential as much of the stock is definitely more cheap than chic. A number of haberdashery and material stalls – as well as the excellent Barney's Textile Centre – also offer D.I.Y. fashion bunnies the chance to create some pretty ritzy outfits with intricate Chinese brocade at £10 a yard, African wax-prints at £7 a yard, linen at £9 a yard. Cheap wools, cottons and off-cuts go for much less. Hats and hair accessories are also well stocked and trainers high profile, with a number of stalls offering some seriously persuasive bargains on brand name ranges: many Nike, Adidas and Reebok styles go for under £30. Sundays also provide the chance to kit out your garden or window box on the cheap, as a high tide of very reasonably priced plants washes into Blackwood Street, half way along the market – pick up trays of Busy Lizzies or daisy bushes for under a fiver.

Once you've battled through the bargains, East Street isn't short of culinary pit stops. Right along its length, the market is dotted with pubs, stalls and cafés: local favourites are Roffo's and Marie's which do a busy trade in sandwiches, milky coffee and fry ups. In a quieter position at the end of the stalls, 'Er in Dawes dishes up a combination of Caribbean and greasy spoon classics (next, incidentally, to the site of London's first birth control clinic). If you want more than a quick bite The Oasis Café on the Walworth Road (on the right, 2 mins from East Street, heading south) does good Turkish dishes for under a fiver.

Getting a Stall
For further details contact Southwark Council (see appendix).

ELEPHANT & CASTLE, SE1

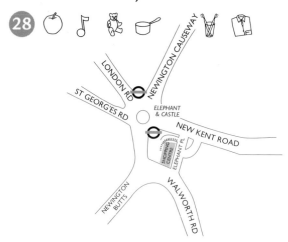

Outside Elephant & Castle shopping centre.
Tube: *Elephant & Castle (Northern and Bakerloo)*
BR: Elephant & Castle (Blackfriars)
Buses: *12, 35, 45, 53, 63, 68, 155, 168, 171, 172, 176, 188, 199, 322, 344, C10, X53, X68*
Open: *Monday-Saturday 9.30am-5pm*

This market, which circles at below ground level outside the
famous shopping centre at Elephant and Castle, has only been up
and running for the last couple of years. Unfortunately, its location
– stuck under the centre's concrete petticoats with the smell of the
municipal toilet never far away – hasn't helped to establish much of
an atmosphere. People surfacing out of the labyrinthine tunnels
under Elephant's twin roundabouts seem mainly concentrated on
getting either to or from work or in or out of Tesco Metro, so you
don't feel very encouraged to potter. The selection of goods on
offer is pretty uninspiring, concentrating on new clothes,
sportswear, accessories, jewellery, watches, toys, electrical and household goods and toiletries – you might find the odd genuine bargain
if you persevere.

On the sartorial front, some stalls stock slightly more interesting and fashionable women's clothes, but the emphasis is on cheap, functional separates aimed generally at a more middle-aged customer. A few traders have £1 rails or jumble-style trestles with mixes of second-hand clothes, but there are few choice items in amongst the nylon nasties of yesteryear. Probably the best things about the market are the three lively food stalls, selling either Thai, Caribbean or African snacks, and the CD stall which does genuinely cheap deals on a good selection of both chart music for £9.99 and back catalogue albums for £4.99.

Although the market isn't worth a special visit, if you do happen to pass through and have time to kill, take a quick look in the shopping centre itself. It may be a much-maligned classic of soulless retail architecture, but Elephant's infamous centrepiece hides a few things that counter the general tone of strip-lit blandness. Opposite Woolworth's, Tlon Books stocks a surprisingly comprehensive selection of competitively priced second-hand fiction and non-fiction titles, catering well for people on the look out for the idiosyncratic as well as the classic. Plus, if you're after a snack, the shopping centre has two tempting options: firstly, the Oasis, an unpretentious little café with admirable ambitions to offer that little something more (grapefruit is a complimentary starter with all greasy spoon options); and a Latin American snack bar which serves cheap, authentic stomach fillers to the strains of salsa, available at the specialist CD stockist in a nearby unit.

Getting a Stall

For further details about getting a stall phone 020 7708 2313

EXMOUTH MARKET, EC1

*Exmouth Market on the junction of
Farringdon Road and Rosebery Avenue.*
Tube: *Farringdon (Circle, Metropolitan)*
Buses: *19, 38, 63, 341*
Open: *Tuesday-Thursday 9.30am-4.30pm*

Exmouth Market has changed almost beyond recognition in the last
few years as cafés and expensive gift and antique shops have moved
onto the street. Unfortunately this has not helped the street market
which has dwindled to just a few stalls selling junk, fruit and veg
and picture frames. The junk stall is usually interesting, but not
worth going too far out of your way to visit.

Getting a stall
For further details contact Islington Council (see appendix)

FARRINGDON ROAD, EC1

Farringdon Road EC1
Closed in 1994.

Farringdon Road was the site of the famous "Bookseller's Row" for
most of this century. It was a great place to find collectable or just
interesting old hardbacks and became an established part of the
London book trade. Although the market largely dealt in the books
discarded by the large auction houses, occasionally a valuable work
would slip through the net. In the early eighties a volume by
Thomas More was bought here for less than £100, which later sold
at Sotheby's for £43,000. By the early nineties George Jeffery was
the last trader doing business here, as had his father and his grandfa-
ther. He had worked here for over forty years since returning from
the war and the terrible British weather and increasingly heavy
traffic were taking their toll on his health. In 1994 Mr Jeffery died
and with him Farringdon Market closed, turning Farringdon Road
into just another busy London street.

GREENWICH, SE10

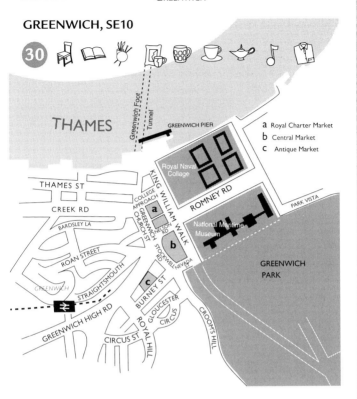

THAMES

Greenwich Foot Tunnel

GREENWICH PIER

a Royal Charter Market
b Central Market
c Antique Market

THAMES ST

CREEK RD

BARDSLEY LA

ROAN STREET

GREENWICH

STRAIGHTSMOUTH

GREENWICH HIGH RD

KING WILLIAM WALK

COLLEGE APPROACH

GREENWICH CHURCH ST

NELSON RD

STOCKWELL RD

NEVADA

BURNEY ST

GLOUCESTER

CIRCUS ST

ROYAL HILL

CIRCUS

GLOUCESTER

Royal Naval College

ROMNEY RD

National Maritime Museum

PARK VISTA

GREENWICH PARK

CROOMS HILL

Greenwich Church Street, Stockwell Street, Greenwich High Road.
BR: *Greenwich (London Bridge), Island Gardens (Docklands Light
Railway – take foot tunnel to Greenwich)*
Buses: *177,180, 188, 199, 286, 386, 108*
River Boat: *This is a great way to see the Thames and visit the market.
There are riverboats running from Westminster, Embankment and Tower pier
every Sunday to Greenwich. For details contact Greenwich Tourist Office on
020 8858 6376*
Open: *Saturday–Sunday 9.30am-5pm,*
Wednesday-Friday 9am-5pm (Crafts Market within the Charter Market)
Thursday 9.30am-5pm (Collectables Market within the Charter Market)

Greenwich is still one of London's largest and most popular Sunday markets, but it seems to have lost its edge in recent years. In the early nineties it looked as though the market on a Sunday would be as big as Camden. The reasons for Greenwich's dwindling popularity are numerous but two key factors have been the take-off of Spitalfields Market as a major tourist attraction (see page 158) and some ill-considered changes to Greenwich Market itself – more of which later. Nonetheless it's still a great market to visit with lots of books, clothing, furniture, music, arts and crafts and antiques scattered among its various sites.

One thing that Greenwich has in abundance and which has endured is its unique atmosphere which, on a busy Sunday, is something like a cross between Portobello Market and Brighton seafront. Its location next to the Thames is the reason for this. If you have time, take a walk to the Greenwich Observatory which offers an incredible view accross the Thames Valley with Canary Wharf and the City in the foreground.

Greenwich

The Royal Charter Market (formerly the Crafts Market)

Greenwich Church Street, College Approach,
King William Walk, Nelson Road
Open: *Thursday 7.30am-5pm Antiques and Collectables,*
Wednesday, Friday-Sunday 9.30-5pm Arts and Crafts

This market is housed in a very grand wrought iron building which was for over one hundred years a fruit and veg market and still has enshrined above the main entrance:

A FALSE BALANCE IS ABOMINATION TO THE LORD BUT A JUST WEIGHT IS HIS DELIGHT

These days the market is given over to arts and crafts at the weekend and, although this term is sometimes used to describe tacky novelty goods that could accurately be regarded as an abomination to the Lord, most of the things here are good value and of reasonable quality. There are quite a few stalls selling clothes made by London designers and one recently offered hand-made suede jackets for only £40, while another sold very good quality leather jackets for only £120; there were also a few stalls selling smart kid's clothes for those with children in tow. There are a fair number of stalls selling things for the home with quite a few dealing in rugs and one specialising in cushions and throws. This market is also a good place to find gifts with a wide range of jewellery on offer, from conventional to more hippy/pagan items, plus several stalls selling scented soaps and another specialising in wonderful wood boxes for as little as £35. There are also a number of photographers selling their framed prints. A welcome recent addition is the deli stall selling olives and fine cheeses.

One of the best things about this market is its relaxed atmosphere and numerous eating and drinking venues. Among the places to sit and relax with a pint and your purchases are The Coach and Horses and Admiral Hardy pubs, or try the Meeting House Café, the trendy new Time Bar or the small patisserie Ciao (which does a great cappaccino). Within the market is a great retro furniture shop called Toot which is well worth a browse.

Greenwich

The antiques and collectables market held here on a Thursday is ideal if you want to avoid the Sunday crowds. About fifty stalls set up here selling all kinds of things such as cheap paperbacks, classical CD's from £4, lots of interesting old toys and all kinds of collectables from seventies kitsch articles to Russian oil paintings from the thirties. Compared to weekends, on a Thursday the market is very quiet with stall holders reading the papers or chatting with an occasional customer and plenty of free tables at The Meeting House Café. Among the bargains recently found here were a solid dark framed mirror for £10 and a good-as-new fifties shirt for only £4.

Getting a Stall

For further details contact the market office on 020 8293 3110, or try the company's head office on 020 7515 7153.

The Central Market

Stockwell Street

Open: *Saturday-Sunday 9am-5pm*

This is the largest market in Greenwich and still a great place to visit, but it has suffered in the last few years due to a misjudged revamp by the management. Until 1994 there was an excellent indoor book market which attracted people from all over London, then the management closed it, decorated it in the worst possible taste (with painted Corinthian arches and vine leaves) and renamed it the Village Market Antique Centre. It is now full of rather strange furniture and the top floor is almost empty, with hardly anything that could be described as an antique. The market that surrounds this building has suffered as a result with much fewer visitors and some vacant stalls. The South London Book Centre is still going strong and well worth a visit. To the side and behind the book centre the market retains some of its former glory, with many of the excellent retro clothing and furniture stalls still trading and Thai and Indian food stalls still serving delicious grub. Towards the back of the market is an indoor complex of stalls with more good quality retro clothing and some fairly expensive, but good quality furniture.

A recent development has been the creation of a narrow arcade connecting this market with King William Walk, but the passage itself is given over to the sale of tourist tat.

The market is much quieter on a Saturday, but does have the added attraction of some organic food stalls selling all kinds of organic produce, from fresh meat to fruit and veg, as well as an excellent bread stall and one specialising in herbs, spices and different varieties of olive oil.

Getting a Stall

To get a stall at the Central Market just turn up by 8.30am and ask to speak to Frank the market manager. For a stall at the Village Market Antiques Centre phone 0956 364 312.

Greenwich Antiques Market

Greenwich High Road (next to the Cinema)
Open: *Saturday and Sunday 9am-5pm*

Despite its name, this market has all kinds of things on offer. Among the fifty or so stalls that set up here on a Sunday (the market is smaller on Saturdays) there are good value retro clothes, very fine new and antique bed linen, antique cutlery, some interesting pieces of furniture, reasonable value paperbacks, a stall specialising in framed mirrors, all kinds of jewellery and several stalls dealing in old postcards, coins and other collectables. The market is open air, which does make it vulnerable to the weather, but on a fine day it is one of the best parts of the market. Among the bargains recently found here were a solid little bookshelf for only £16 and a selection of funky T-shirts for only £2.50 each. This section is not as well known as other parts of the market, the stall holders are usually prepared to barter and there are always bargain rails here selling garments to clear. Next door to the market is the Studio Bar which also serves snacks and has seating outside in clement weather.

Getting a Stall

For further details about Greenwich Antiques market contact Jane on 020 7237 1318.

OFF TO MARKET FOR FASHION FOOD & FUN!

Visit two South-of-the-River classics, and a central London newcomer

GREENWICH - THE ROYAL CHARTER MARKET

Historic Georgian covered space in the heart of the Millennium village, en route from Sark to Park. One of London's oldest markets with some of London's newest things - arts and crafts, gifts and décor. Open Wednesday, Friday, Saturday and Sunday, with antiques on Thursdays.

Enquiries 020 8293 3110.

MERTON ABBEY MILLS RIVERSIDE SHOPPING VILLAGE

Lovely day out in a picturesque corner of Wimbledon. Crafts and gifts market, with delicious eats, children's theatre and historic working waterwheel every Saturday and Sunday; shops, pub and restaurant open weekdays too; antiques Thursday mornings, car bootsale Saturday mornings. On A24 Merantun Way, nearest tube station Colliers Wood.

Enquiries 020 8543 9608.

And now...PLATFORM 12 AT KING'S CROSS

Latest in a famous family of markets, new marketplace and shopping village for travellers, workers and locals, right between St Pancras and King's Cross Stations, open all day Thursday and Friday.

Enquiries 020 7837 5982.

HAMMERSMITH ROAD, W6

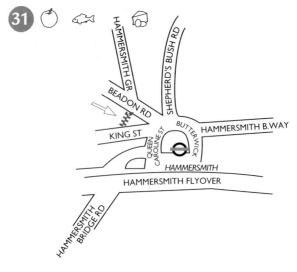

At the bottom end of Hammersmith Grove,
between King Street and Beadon Road
Tube: *Hammersmith (Hammersmith & City, Piccadilly and District)*
Buses: *9, 10, 27, 33, 72, 209, 211, 220, 283, 295, 391*
Open: *Monday-Saturday 9am-5pm*

Despite having been shunted around a number of times in the last few decades by local redevelopment, Hammersmith Grove's seven or so regular stalls are still going strong in a now well-established site nestling beside the hefty concrete flanks of King's Mall. The setting isn't up to much, but the market still has enough charisma to make it worth a detour off the high street, where you can join locals in stocking up on a solid selection of fruit and veg, shellfish and eggs – occasionally household goods are also on sale. John Tydeman's stall (in the family since the 1890's) gleams with a pick-'n'mix of fish and, for as little as 50p, you can select a sill-brightener from the raft of cheerful flowers offered by the bedding plants lady.

The lively Broadway Snack Bar (on the market precinct) is the best bet for a rest, and with its Formica-cladding and stem stools is a great place for retro-purists in search of the smeared authenticity of a real coffee joint. Highly recommended by traders and local shop-keepers as a proper, "no burgers" restaurant, the Broadway staff serve up coffees (40p), boiled bacon dinners, sandwiches and breakfasts with genuine friendliness as locals and traders squeeze in and out for a chat. The florist on Beadon Street is also worth a quick visit: with its Victorian frontage and flower-crammed windows, Turner's is a postcard-perfect remnant of London's commercial past.

Getting a Stall
For further details contact Hammersmith & Fulham Council (see appendix).

HAMPSTEAD COMMUNITY MARKET, NW3

Hampstead Community Centre, 78 Hampstead High Street.
Tube: *Hampstead (Northern)*
Buses: *46, 268*
Open: *Saturday-Sunday 10am-6pm, and Bank Holidays*

The only compelling reason to pay a visit to this market is to get a drink without having to cram into one of Hampstead's homogenised, over-priced coffee bars. Beverages and homemade cakes are consumed sitting on school chairs arranged around a little cluster of tables which makes a nice hideout in which to escape the gorgeous hoards of the High Street.

Housed in what looks like a miniature village hall, the market is an oasis of the slightly naff – an effective antidote to NW3's air of well-groomed uniformity. The greatest hits of the craft fayre: painted glassware, batik cards, decorated wood photo frames, hand-made soaps – all put in an appearance, backed up by homeopathic oils and unimaginative jewellery. Clothes are all ethno-print head-mistress chic and the bric-à-brac, predominantly of the glove-stretchers and delicate hankies ilk. Things are generally over-priced. That said, a recent visit bagged a 1950's Italian two-tone vase for only £2, so the odd bargain can obviously pop up. And the market does have a dash of character, retaining a community spirit Hampstead High Street often seems to have lost: friends chat next to racks stuffed with local information leaflets or pass the time of day with the tea ladies. Like the goods inside the market, the fruit, fish and nuts stalls which flank it in an adjacent passage aren't going to pull in punters from outside the immediate area. Produce is top-notch: scrubbed, beautiful and no doubt delicious – but all at NW3 prices.

You might have more fun across the road at 'Exclusivo', a second-hand designer clothes shop. Ignore the dreadful Euro-tat name and head on in for a good rummage. Hampstead may not have bargain veg, but it does offer a better class of cast-off: you can find garments by groovy names like Dries Van Noten or Alexander McQueen for under £60, amongst racks crammed with coats, dresses, and separates.

Getting a Stall
For further details contact the community centre on 020 7794 8313.

Hampstead Community Market

HILDRETH STREET, SW12

Hildreth Street.
Tube: *Balham (Northern)*
BR: *Balham*
Buses: *155, 315, 355 (Balham High Road)*
Open: *Monday-Saturday 9.30am-5pm, Wednesdays until 1pm*

Balham Market has been located in this pedestrianised corridor between grand Toblerone-roofed Victorian buildings since the turn of the century, but is now probably a shadow of its former self with less than a dozen stalls. Despite its slightly neglected atmosphere, this small provisions market is doing well to survive in the shadow of big hitters Safeways and Sainsburys who fight it out on either side of the High Road.

Hildreth Street market acts mainly as a supplement to a row of shops aimed at supplying the needs of Balham's Afro-Caribbean community. A choice of grocery units means that it's a good place to stock up cheaply on things like pulses, herbs, spices and more adventurous vegetables and you can get specialist breads or patties from the busy bakery. There's an excellent range of fish on offer in the street, with exotic varieties such as yellow croakers available alongside more standard options, in either of two separate fishmongers. Other shops sell African music, cosmetics, and hair accessories. You're not going to find anything too exciting on the stalls themselves, but as a whole the market does a good job of providing cheap food to a steady flow of local shoppers. One stall sells tropical fruit (limes and mangoes are well-priced) while the rest specialise in conventional British fruit and veg. Although these four stalls have nothing particularly flash on offer, the range of combined stock is quite impressive, with more unusual indigenous varieties of apples and old-fashioned berries stacked alongside lots of feisty-looking greens. The rest of the market is made up of stalls selling utility classics: eggs, cards, socks and underwear, as well as wildcard specialisms like flip-flops for £1.

Although Balham Market doesn't really warrant a special trip, if you do find yourself in Hildreth Street the immediate area has a few other attractions stashed away. Together, the local cafés offer a good range of greasy spoon experiences: on Bedford Hill, Laila's dishes up slightly upmarket (pasta is on the menu) breakfasts and lunches while, a few doors up, Smiley's does the no-frills version. But it's Dot's on Hildreth Street which wins the purist vote with its floor-fixed blue seating, peeling posters of Turkey and gleaming period piece coffee machines. At the top of Hildreth Street, turn right onto Bedford Hill for a further dose of retro in Etienne's, a crammed junk shop specialising in French café-style furniture and accessories: elegant wooden chairs start at a fiver.

Getting a Stall

For further details contact Wandsworth Council (see appendix).

HOXTON STREET, N1

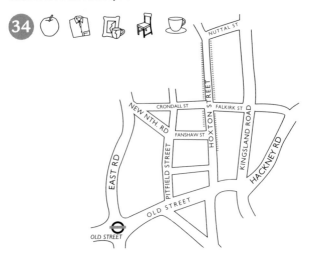

Hoxton Street, between Falkirk Street and Nuttall Street.
Tube: *Old Street (Northern)*
BR: *Old Street*
Buses: *55 (Old Street); 67, 149, 242 (Kingsland Road)*
Open: *Monday-Saturday 9am-4pm*

Tucked well away from the end of Hoxton recently engulfed by the tide of trendification rolling east from Clerkenwell, Hoxton Market is still doing the old-fashioned job of selling unremarkable but cheap necessities to a local population based around the area's large council estates. During the week, this scruffy street of butchers, cafés, discount stores and bakeries is home to just a handful of stalls selling eggs, fruit and veg, fish and the odd bit of junk. It's on a Saturday that Hoxton Street comes into its own when a forest of rails and tables springs up selling a wide range of (predominantly new) clothes, shoes, household goods and discount food.
Although you are probably not going to find anything fantastic, Hoxton Street does stock an extensive selection of both functional and fashionable garments at prices generally under a tenner.

Capitalise on the best of what's on offer by taking home a low-commitment purchase for a night out (some stalls are good for zeit-geisty high street rip offs, like Chinese-style embroidered skirts for £5, or lace tops for £1.99), a classic shirt (Ben Sherman's go for around £20) or a good, plain T-shirt (£3). Some label-oriented stalls also sell designer goods at sizeable reductions and, put together, the various shoe stalls stock a wide range of both first and second-hand styles: nicely worn in white Italian leather loafers for £8, or fashionable leather boots for £20.

Generally, the rest of the stalls reflect the needs of local inhabitants with the emphasis on food, bedding (duvet covers for around a tenner), pots and pans (second-hand frying pans for £2 and a good selection of cheap metal utensils), toiletries and cosmetics, along with an extensive choice of fruit, veg and fish. The stand-out selection is of children's clothes and toys, which are often extremely cheap (e.g. Mothercare dresses £3), especially towards the north end of the market, where rummage boxes and trestles are full of vests, uniforms, bibs, pyjamas etc. going for as little as 50p. It's also the market's top end which is probably of most interest to junk-seekers, where several stalls offer second-hand bric-à-brac and clothes. Nothing to die for, but the odd glass (from 10p), book (from 20p), piece of crockery or retro shirt (50p) might pop up if you have a thorough pick through everything.

For something to eat, try either F. Cooke for pie 'n' mash, Café des Amis for a baguette sandwich or one of the market's many greasy spoons for a solid lunch (around £3). If you fancy something a bit funkier, head 5 minutes south for a drink or snack in either of two trendy-magnets: the Electricity Showrooms bar (Hoxton Street) or The LUX Bar (Hoxton Square). If you have time pop into the Standpoint Gallery on Coronet Street which stages interesting photography and contemporary art shows or, for cutting edge work with a new technology slant, check out the LEA Gallery in Hoxton Square's LUX Centre.

Getting a Stall

For further details contact Hackney Council (see appendix).

INVERNESS STREET, NW1

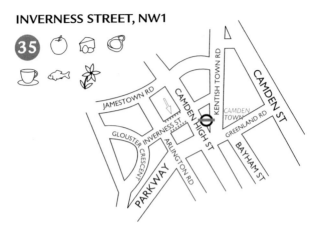

off Camden High Street
Tube: *Camden Town (Northern Line)*
Buses: *24, 27, 31, 168*
Open: *Monday-Saturday 9am-5pm, Thursday 9am-1pm*

This is a great value local market with about ten stalls selling quality fruit and veg, cut flowers, fresh fish, pet food, underwear and novelty souvenirs. The grocery stalls seem to be doing well and have even expanded their range of exotic produce in recent years but, sadly, the excellent cheese stall is no longer here.

What makes this little market special is the fact that it survives alongside the massive Camden Market (see page 38). In fact Inverness Street predates the fashion market by many years, being a throwback to the days before Camden became trendy.

Not really worth going out of your way to visit but, if you are visiting the main market, Inverness Street is a welcome diversion from the teenage throng and is now becoming one of the best places for food and refreshment in Camden. Among the new cafés are the smart Café Solo and the trendy, but always busy, Bar Gansa.

Getting a stall
For further details contact Camden Council (see appendix).

Inverness Street

KILBURN, NW6

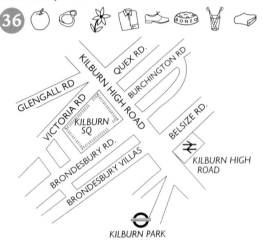

On Kilburn High Road between Brondesbury Road and Victoria Road.
Tube: *Kilburn Park (Bakerloo)*
BR: *Kilburn High Road*
Buses: *16, 28, 32, 98, 189, 206, 316 (Kilburn High Road)*
Open: *Monday-Saturday 9am-5.30pm*

Being stuck beneath an architectural tangle of access walkways that lead to the adjacent residential area and situated next to the grimiest stretch of NW London's arterial road, Kilburn Market (although fairly friendly) isn't the place to head for a pleasant potter. Inside the railings – the complex is a bit uninviting, despite the cheerful blue and yellow livery – a series of lock-up units stock a pretty average range of cheap goods, supplementing the functional selection on offer in the busy high street. Here you can find fruit and veg, African groceries, new clothes, plants and flowers, household goods and toiletries, bedding and towels (the duvet plus pillowcase deals are worth a look), underwear, jewellery, hair accessories, hats, carpets, luggage and bags, kids clothes and electrical goods – in short, the sort of stuff you can get anywhere.

Although in general nothing here warrants a special trip, the market does hold pockets of interest in the form of a discount trainers stall, "Rainbow Fabrics" – a haberdashery crammed full of glitzy fabrics (priced at between £1.50 and £3), whose owner maintains it is one of the few shops left which can give John Lewis a run for its money: "People think the old days are back!" – and twin pet-care units, the One Step Shop and Paul's Aquatic World. If you ever doubted the market viability of consumer goods for gerbils, think again: One Step stocks a plethora of treats, homes, beds, toys and vanity products, without ignoring timeless favourites like the squeaky ball and novelty bone. Next door, Paul's houses wall to wall tanks, with an impressive range of both tropical and freshwater fish, with prices starting at £1 for a goldfish to £20 plus for more exotic types – a "Discus", "Silver Dollar" or "Bumble Bee" can all be bagged up for you.

Decent refreshments are thin on the ground here, although Kabul John's in the far right hand corner of the market serves up standard greasy-spoon fare. Alternatively, in the hope of sampling a bit of authentic Irish atmosphere, you could try your luck in one of Kilburn's many pubs. But if only civilised dining will do, a trip to down to the south end of the High Road at number 45 is well worth it as the tastefully restrained French restaurant, Le Marseille, offers authentic three course lunches for just £6 – oddly-located it may be, but the Evening Standard's verdict was: "utterly delightful".

Getting a stall

The market is privately run by Graysim Holdings, for further details contact the market manager on 01494 871 277 or 0468 206 754.

KINGSLAND WASTE, E8

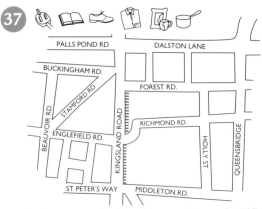

Kingsland Waste, Kingsland Road between Forest and Middleton Road
Rail: *Dalston Junction (Broad Street)*
Buses: *67, 149, 242, 243, 243A*
Open: *Saturday 9am-5pm*

On Saturdays, the wide pavements and parking area alongside
Kingsland Road become a hive of consumer activity as about eighty
stalls set out their wares. The market has a rather seedy reputation
and there are a few shifty characters about, like the one I saw selling
boxed cordless phones from a bag for £10, but such sights are an
exception and only add to the novelty of visiting the place.
Kingsland Waste caters particularly well for DIY enthusiasts, with
many stalls offering brand new hand tools at low prices and one
specialising in used power tools with bargains like a Bosch circular
saw for only £45 (new price around £80). If DIY isn't your thing
there are quite a few new clothes stalls with one offering M&S
T-shirts for £5 and four cotton vests for only £5. Another stall was
doing a brisk trade in designer label clothes of dubious authenticity
with Levi jeans for £20 and Ben Sherman shirts for £12. The stall
selling CD's for £4.99 has a limited stock with no shortage of
rubbish, but along with the Thompson Twins and Chess the Musical,
you may find something of interest or you can just browse and enjoy

the spectacle of the stall holder singing along to his music. The well-organised second-hand shop at numbers 484-486 Kingsland Road complements the market and is definitely worth a browse.

For those looking for more second-hand things, the southern part of the market (south of Richmond Road) has several stalls selling old clothes, electrical goods and bric-à-brac. The market also has a surprisingly good second-hand book stall with hundreds of books randomly spread over tables and crammed into boxes on the floor. Among the bargains I found a hardback edition of the collected works of Dr Johnson for only 80p. This part of the market also has a very cheap fabric stall with many for only £2 a metre.

If you want something to eat or drink after your shopping there are a good few places to choose from including Faulkners for traditional fish and chips (at number 424), next door is Usha for Indian food and further south is Kardesler Restaurant (at number 398) for Turkish cuisine. If you fancy clogging your arteries with traditional British grub there's always the Kingsland Café, but it can get very busy.

Getting a Stall

For further details contact Hackney Council (see appendix).

Kingsland Waste

LEADENHALL, EC3

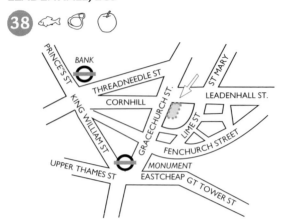

Whittington Avenue, off Gracechurch Street and Leadenhall Street
Tube: *Bank (Central and Northern), Monument (Circle and District)*
Buses: *8, 25, 26, 35, 43, 47, 48, 149, 242*
Open: *Monday-Friday 7am-4pm*

Leadenhall has been the site of a market for nearly six hundred years and in that time it was twice destroyed by fire and rebuilt on several occasions. The grand cast-iron and stone structure that stands today was designed by Sir Horace Jones in 1881 and has a wonderful atmosphere with arched thoroughfares leading to a domed central meeting place. The only hitch in this tale of continuity is the fact that Leadenhall market has evolved to the stage where it is not a market at all, but rather an established shopping arcade containing many high street shops including a branch of Jigsaw and Waterstones. It is still an interesting place to visit and there are several very fine greengrocers, fishmongers and butchers within the arcade which continue to sell the kind of produce that has been sold here for centuries.

Another thing that gives this market a unique character is its location in the heart of London's financial square mile with the Lloyd's building designed by Richard Rodgers looming above it. If you don't enjoy crowds its advisable to avoid this area during lunchtime when thousands of city folk in suits descend upon the market to get something to eat or do a bit of shopping. I would encourage a look at the spectacular steel and glass Lloyds Building from Leadenhall Place you can enjoy the sight of people going up and down the building in the external glass lifts. Leadenhall is an interesting place to visit on any week day but is at its best in the weeks running up to Christmas when the food shops are festooned with seasonal fare.

Getting a Stall
All the stalls at Leadenhall are run on a leasehold basis and not available for short term rent.

Whitecross Street

LEATHER LANE, EC1

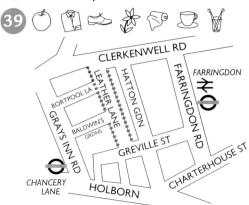

Leather Lane between Clerkenwell Road and Greville Street

Tube: *Farringdon (Circle and Metropolitan), Chancery Lane (Central)*

Buses: *55, 242, 505 (Clerkenwell)*

17, 45, 46, 243, 341 (Gray's Inn Road)

Open: *Monday-Friday 10.30am-2.00pm*

The decline of Exmouth Market and the closure of Farringdon Book Market leaves Leather Lane as the last major market in Clerkenwell. The market gets most of its trade from the nearby office workers of Clerkenwell and Holborn, but there are enough things of interest to make it worth a visit even if you don't work in the area. To avoid the crowds, it's advisable to visit the market between 10.30am and 12 noon before the street fills with people out for a quick shop during their lunch break. The cheap magazine stall on the corner of Clerkenwell Road is a good place to start, with hundreds of slightly out of date mags covering anything from body-building to celebrity gossip for 50p each or 3 for £1. Most of the clothes stalls in this part of the market deal in smart office and some casual wear. The synthetic fur coats for £25 seemed a good buy, as did the tight-fitting women's T-shirts on offer at £15 for two.

Further south, past Portpool Lane, the recent arrival of a small contemporary art gallery is a welcome addition, although the

Leather Lane

wonderful Ferraro Continental Food Store has now closed down. It is in this part of the market (between Portpool Lane and St Cross Street) that some of the most interesting stalls can be found. On a recent visit, a temporary trader was selling stylish metal bowls for £10 and large floor-standing candlestick holders for only £20. Another stall sells street fashion such as bodywarmers, canvas slacks and full-length skirts, all for £10 each. Just opposite the junction with St Cross Street is a charity shop (Camden Age Concern) for those who enjoy bargain hunting. The fabric stall represents excellent value with some large remnants for only a fiver and many fabrics for only £2 per metre. Further along, Leather Lane has one of the best jewellery stalls in London with simple rings for as little as £5. One customer asked for arm bracelets and from behind the stall emerged a box with a variety of funky designs to choose from. There are several good clothing stalls in this area and some pretty impressive bargains to be found, such as the chunky fleece top for only £10. The bedding and towel stall is also good value.

The busiest part of the market is the square of stalls between Beauchamp Gardens and Greville Street. The stall selling mainstream videos for £7.99, Playstation games and children's posters for only £1 is always busy. The cheap foodstuffs pitch is also excellent, offering 3 packets of Dutch butter for only £1 and many continental delicacies such as German sweet cake at well below supermarket prices. It is in this part of the market that children's inflatable chairs and sofas can be found for only £5.

Among the best places to get refreshment after your hectic shop are Collin's Nest and just off the market, on St Cross Street, there's Shorties and an Italian café – all offering basic grub at a good price. If you don't mind eating on the hoof there's also Traditional Plaice for fish and chips and the Bagel Bakery. There are several good shops in the area including L. Terroni & Sons deli on Clerkenwell Road, one of the last reminders of Clerkenwell's fading Italian community.

Getting a Stall
For further details contact Camden Council (see appendix).

LEWISHAM HIGH STREET, SE13

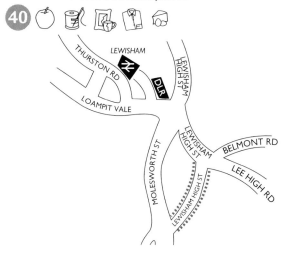

Along the north end of Lewisham High Street.
BR: *Lewisham or Ladywell*
(Charing Cross, Waterloo and London Bridge)
Buses: *21, 36, 180 225, 380, 47, 54, 75, 136, 185, 199, 208*
(Lewisham High Street)
Open: *Monday-Saturday 9am-5pm (General Market);*
Monday 6am-1pm (Bric-a-brac Fair).

Hemmed in by chainstores and flanking the "everything under one roof" Lewisham Centre, this functional market nonetheless appears to be holding its own. Even on a weekday, a steady flow of shoppers along this pedestrianised section of the High Street creates pockets of friendly chit-chat as locals cruise the line of stalls offering standard market fare and cheap food. Although unremarkable, the market's jaunty, bulb-lit stalls and sprinklings of old-time banter make it a fun place to stock up on groceries: a number of fruit and veg stalls offer a wide selection, with the remainder selling flowers, fish, eggs, new clothes, watches, household goods, cheap ornaments, underwear, cards, make-up and haberdashery.

Every Monday, a small bric-à-brac fair makes a stand for idiosyncracy amidst the blandness of the Lewisham Centre. Located at the south end, in a hall on the Molesworth Road side (beyond the main entrance of C&A) the fair's mix of low-octane antiques, new crafts and near junk is only really worth a quick pick through, but the cluster of stalls selling period jewellery have some interesting and unusual pieces.

Getting a stall

For further details contact Lewisham Council (see appendix). The bric-à-brac fair is privately run, for more information phone John on 01426 924 201.

Lewisham High Street

LOWER MARSH, SE1

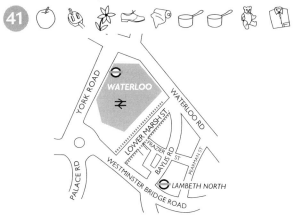

Lower Marsh from Westminster Bridge Road to Baylis Road.
Tube: *Waterloo (Northern, Bakerloo, Waterloo & City),*
Lambeth North (Bakerloo)
BR: *Waterloo (take the exit nearest Platform 1, follow the road down and take the underpass into Leake Street).*
Buses: *1, 188, 68, X68, 168, 171, 176 (Waterloo Road);*
12, 53, 76, 109, 171A (Westminster Bridge Road)
Open: *Monday-Friday from around 9am, with market fully operational over lunchtime: 11am-2pm; some stall holders also set up on Saturdays, but the market is a lot more patchy.*

Having been forcibly down-sized by the demise of the GLC in the eighties (which knocked out a considerable chunk of lunchtime trade), Lower Marsh is no longer the large, vibrant market it was when it used to stretch right into The Cut. Despite this, traders on this site have over 150 years of tradition to uphold and the market certainly doesn't look in danger of terminal decline, as every day a reliable influx of shoppers fills the narrow street. As with most community markets, utility is the name of the game at Lower Marsh with traders focusing on everyday needs: fruit and veg, household goods and kitchen equipment (check out the deals on pan sets and knives), toiletries, haberdashery and material, luggage, children's games and toys, as well as electrical items like personal stereos, radios and cameras. Underwear and socks, bedding plants and flowers, sweets, cards, batteries, women's office wear, shoes, hair accessories, CDs (new releases £11.99), bedding and towels all get a look in too. There are also a few stalls selling African crafts, craft materials and jewellery, and maverick specialists stocking single lines like Telly Tubby merchandise, and steel rulers.

EuroStar day-trippers and tourists tend to head north for the civic grandeur of the South Bank complex rather than opt to explore the rumbling, grimy streets at the back of Waterloo, but Lower Marsh is well worth a visit for a slice of London at its hybrid best. The street itself is probably more of a pull than the market as waves of commercial development have left a lively blend of trendy boutiques, specialist businesses and traditional, functional shops: gents outfitters L&C Cohen (trading since 1921) coexists happily with Honour, a rubber store whose window comes on all Soho with its basques, chains and feathers.

Clothing is one of Lower Marsh's fortes, with a number of both first and second-hand shops; try retro boutique Radio Days for impeccably suave clothes, furniture and ephemera, and What The Butler Wore for racks full of stylishly synthetic fifties-to-seventies clothes. Prophet jewellers is also worth a look for unusual contemporary jewellery and 20/20 Vision stocks designer frames at well under West End prices. Other interesting units include the well-established classical music shop, Gramex, and the Far East Supermarket, which stocks everything from pak choi to tom yum, as well as great spices and strange packets of things like Great Impression "losing weight" tea.

When it comes to eating, Lower Marsh has an option for everyone. Food stops mirror the hybrid mix of shops, with the range running from Thai to greasy spoon – Marie's Café is the best for retro fans – and for foodies, Deli-Rium offers gorgeous breads, cheeses and meats as well as light lunches. Further afield on Cornwall Road, "bespoke bakery" Konditor & Cook is crammed with lovingly-crafted cakes, breads and sandwiches and also has a concession in the Young Vic on The Cut if you fancy a sit down treat. The cavernous Fire Station Bar on Waterloo Road serves solid lunches, or you can opt for take out from Coopers Natural Foods (on Lower Marsh), an old-school "stripped pine and pasties" health food shop.

Getting a Stall
For further details contact Lambeth Council (see appendix).

Lower Marsh

MERTON ABBEY MILLS, SW19

Off Merantun Way, Behind the Savacentre, South Wimbledon
Tube: *Colliers Wood (Northern)*
Buses: *57, 152, 155, 200*
Open: *Saturday-Sunday 10am-5pm,*
Thursday 6am-12pm (antiques and collectables)

Merton Abbey Mills gives the impression of being very old, but in fact only the Watermill and The Colourhouse dates from the 18th century. The other buildings in the complex were constructed in the early 20th century, and followed the principles of William Morris's Arts and Crafts Movement under the patronage of Arthur Liberty who founded the eponymous Regent Street store. The buildings were originally used as workshops, but fell into disuse and dereliction, only being restored and turned into a retail location in 1989. It is an attractive place to shop particularly with the River Wandle flowing by its side, although the Savacentre with its large car park and the busy road system around it, detracts a little from its charm.

The market itself is best visited on Sundays when nearly two hundred stalls set up here. It's a good place to find new clothes with a fair mix of fashion, smart casual and kids wear, but there are perhaps a few too many stalls selling tie dye and general hippy stuff for most people's liking. The indoor market (known as the Long Shop) has some excellent craft stalls with one woman hand painting gift cards for £2.50 and another selling good quality leather belts and bags for under £20. The artist selling his colourful abstract canvasses from £35 was good value as was the stall selling beautiful bonsai trees for £12. A recent visit also uncovered a stall with stylish lava lamps for only £25 which were a great buy. As with the clothes, it's very much a case of sorting the wheat from the chaff, with a great deal of novelty rubbish like the stall selling candles in the form of a naked woman with unfeasibly large breasts (an offense to good taste and a waste of wax to my mind).

One of the best things about the market is the number of good shops that have a permanent location here. It's particularly good for second-hand books with several established bookshops on the site offering anything from expensive first editions to comics, and all of them extending their stock onto the pavement on market days. For gifts, herbs and other craft items, the long established Greencades stands out as the best shop on site and has expanded its premises since the last edition of this book.

There is also an antiques and collectables market held here on Thursdays in the Long Shop which has about fifty stalls and is a regular visiting place for London dealers. As with other similar markets such as Bermondsey and Camden Passage, it's a good idea to get here early.

If you're in need of refreshment after your shopping there is the Abbey Mills Gallery Café which serves terrific coffee and has seating outside. The Gourmet Pizza restaurant is good if you want a meal and there is also the William Morris free house towards the back of the market if you fancy a pint. If you don't mind eating on the move the far end of the market has all kinds of food stalls serving anything from Thai curries to roast pork sandwiches.

Getting a Stall

For further details about a stall at the weekend phone 020 8543 9608. If you would like a stall at the Thursday antiques and collectables market phone 0836 581 422.

NAG'S HEAD, N7

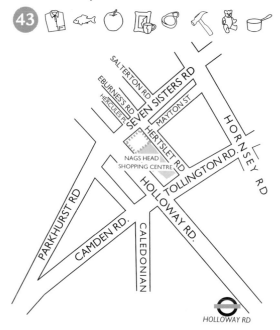

South side of Seven Sisters Road,
just beyond the junction with Holloway Road.
Tube: *Holloway Road (Piccadilly Line)*
Bus: *4, 29, 91, 153, 253, 259, 279 (Seven Sisters Road) ;*
17, 43, 271 (Holloway Road)
Open: *Monday-Saturday 9am-5pm, Sunday 7am-2pm (busiest days*
Wednesday and Saturday)

Nag's Head market suffers from being stuck next to a grotty road
junction and having to fight for attention with the anonymous
brightness of the area's many fast food chains. Things haven't been
improved by the recent transformation of the eponymous Nag's
Head into a sanitised Irish theme pub with the full range of "Celtic
by numbers" clichés. Despite these handicaps, the market's friendly,

community atmosphere is still intact, with piped pop music and all-weather roof offering the opportunity for a cheerful rain-free wander. The market's entrance is lined with permanent stalls: fruit and veg, fish, new clothes, CDs & tapes (cheap, but skewed towards Crooners 'n' Swooners), artificial flowers, and bulk-buy biscuits and sweets. Beyond this is the roofed section with a small café and rotating pitches that change according to the day of the week. A no-frills mix of the professional and amateur means there are plenty of bargains dotted about in the range of goods, with a different emphasis daily: on Mondays, Tuesdays and Thursdays the focus is on new and second-hand clothes and bric-à-brac (including jewellery, toys and books); on Wednesdays the goods are exclusively second-hand; on Fridays and Saturdays the focus is on brand new merchandise and there's a general flea market every Sunday. Generic market services and clobber (household goods, key-cutting, meat, shoes, general gifts etc.) are also mixed in throughout the week. The second-hand clothes on Wednesdays are good, democratically ranging from 50p to £50, with a lot of solid reductions on flasher designer labels (a Valentino shirt for £4) and rails well worth a rummage for cheap retro items. Overall, a good place for periodic pottering.

Traders recommend nearby Hercules Street (north of the market) for refuelling, with the Hercules Café, and Manoli's Grills and Snacks with its Greek-Cypriot-meets-greasy-spoon fare, offering two chances to eat on the cheap. There is nothing much else to inspire in the immediate area, except the excellent Fresco Fisheries shop at No.60 Seven Sisters Road, which has an impressive range of international catches.

Getting a stall

For further details contact the market manager, Bill Willingham on 020 7607 3527.

NEW COVENT GARDEN, SW8

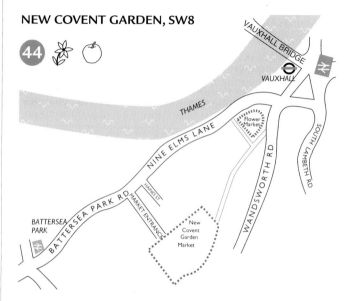

At Vauxhall end of the site between Nine Elms Lane and Wandsworth Road. [NB: the pedestrian entrance to the flower market is opposite the road crossing over the Nine Elms Road junction, hidden up some stairs into what looks like an office complex.]

Cars visiting the market are charged £2 per visit.

BR: *Vauxhall (Victoria)*

Buses: *44, 344 (Nine Elms Lane); 77, 77a, 322 (Wandsworth Road)*

Open: *Monday-Friday 3am-10.30am, Saturday 7am-9am*

NB: the best days are apparently Monday and Thursday because fresh deliveries are made the night before – and Saturday is bargain day, where things are cleared before the traders' day off.

Sited in the middle of one of the most unglamorous stretches of riverside in Central London, New Covent Garden Market is an enormous, ugly complex stranded in a concrete wasteland, carved up by roads full of noisy vans and hemmed in by rattling train lines. But don't let this put you off – utility on this vast a scale was never going to be pretty. Purpose built in the early seventies to replace the famous fruit, veg and flower market at Covent Garden in WC2, this wholesale operation is the engine of London's fresh provisions industry and a great early morning destination for those interested in seeing a hidden side of the working capital.

The fruit and vegetable market on the western end of the site is a monumental cluster of over 200 numbered lock-ups centred round an aisle strewn with food casualties and criss-crossed by fork-lift trucks. The massive quantities of produce involved mean that selling to the public is out of the question and although no one is actually hostile, shunting 100 weight of turnips isn't much of a spectator sport. Try and have a quick look, because the sheer size of the operation is pretty impressive (as is the view of the market's neighbour, Battersea Power Station, at the far end of the complex), but this part of the site certainly has limited appeal for those set on rooting out early morning bargains.

New Covent Garden

There are buckets, literally, of these in the nearby flower market, and the smell is a lot more appealing. Housed in a huge warehouse – lorries docked around its perimeter and inside – it has the character of an Eastern Bloc airport departure lounge. The architecture might be clinical, but the colourful sea of flowers and plants you overlook as you arrive on the first floor terrace is anything but: banked boxes, tables, buckets and trays are carpeted with what seems like every imaginable kind of bloom, bedding plant or bush.

Not all the traders sell to the public, but the vast majority will happily supply you with a carryable amount of flowers for at least half the price of florists or supermarkets – blooms tend to be sold in multiples of bunches, e.g. 10 bunches of irises (around 50) for £7, or by the bucket. In amongst the more serious punters there are plenty of members of the public buying in this way, so don't be shy. New Covent Garden Market is the perfect place to deck out a wedding, or seriously impress the one you love – the hard bit is choosing what you want. Just wandering around is great fun: some of the blooms are incredibly exotic.

You can also get bedding plants, but as one trader advised: "the smaller the unit, the more you have to buy", so make sure you haven't bought enough to kit out Kew Gardens before you start someone boxing up pots of pansies. Small trees and bushes are also dotted around, as well as unusual decorative accessories such as sprays of fresh chillies, sections of bamboo and other unorthodox branches and berries; you can also find designer gardening supplies like aluminium planters and watering cans at large reductions on West End prices. The terracotta pot outlet at the western side of the market is well worth a visit, with baby ones at only 50p, and more hefty models (suitable for say bay trees, or small conifers) going for around £30-£40. The satisfaction of getting all this stuff so cheap is almost as heady as the amassed scents of the thousands of flowers. The flower market has two cafés. The one on the gallery level has a surprisingly expensive greasy spoon menu, so it's probably best to stay downstairs with Tony's Refreshments, which dishes up cheaper versions of the same kind of thing for nattering traders.

NINE ELMS SUNDAY MARKET, SW8

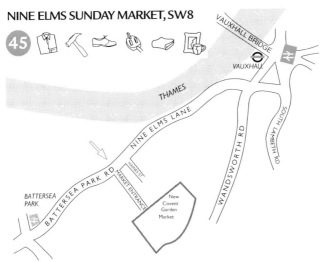

The market is sited inside New Covent Garden Market, but on a Sunday, pedestrians can't access it through the flower market complex to the north. The easiest way to get in is to follow Nine Elms Lane south for about 10 minutes, and then turn into the market's access road when you reach the Booker Cash & Carry depot on your left.

BR: *Battersea Park*

Buses: *44, 344 (Nine Elms Lane); 77, 77a, 322 (Wandsworth Road)*

Open: *Sunday 9am-2pm*

As markets go, Nine Elms isn't at all bad. It has lots of stalls selling the sort of utility classics that street markets do best, a lively atmosphere and plenty of decent bric-à-brac to pick over on the car-boot stalls which share its pitch space. The problem is its location. Because it's sited in the central row of what during the week is New Covent Garden vegetable market, gaining access to Nine Elms can for dwarfed pedestrians feel like trying to pick your way across a cross-channel ferry depot. Once you've slogged up the access road, through the underpass, across a slip road and found a gap in the car park wall, then skinnied between a few lorry bumpers and located the right access arch – the sight of human life inside the market is a real relief.

And there is plenty of it: tides of people move round the large circuit of stalls in a rough-and-ready atmosphere stoked by loud music stalls and the combined fairground waft of fastfood vans. Nine Elms offers no real suprises as about half the stalls sell new clothes and shoes while the remainder offer a range of standard market clobber including kitchenware, bedding, toys, fake flowers, plants, plastic bits and pieces, towels and some fairly dodgy ornaments. The clothes are incredibly cheap, with nothing much over £5. The catch is the quality. You might get the odd bargain on a pair of trainers or Birkenstock-style sandals, but there's not much to tempt anyone after something to wear from the ankles up. The ranges seem to concentrate on either mumsy dresses or barely-there teen fashions. But as with all markets, the piles of boxer shorts, ladies underwear and socks are worth a rummage for cheap and cheerful cotton staples.

Cheap fruit and veg (a large bowl of peppers for £1) and a stall selling pastries and bread (5 doughnuts for £1) could make a trip worthwhile if you lived locally, and one stallholder sells a range of interesting-looking Mediterranean cheeses. Nine Elms also has a good selection of DIY stalls that offer serious reductions on bewildering arrays of vital tools and gismos, plus most have £1 tables full of useful bits and bobs like stick-on hooks and heavy-duty tape. The CD stall has a surprisingly broad and up-to-date range of music, selling chart titles for just £10.

If you don't fancy an old-school burger or hot-dog then you could try the Market Café (under the access arches to your left as you enter the market) for a no-frills greasy brunch. Also have a look at the car-boot pitches to the right of the entrance. Although much of the stuff on sale is only a whisker away from skip fodder, there are a few people offering decent retro kitchenware, clocks and small bits of furniture.

Getting a Stall

This market is privately run, for more details contact Bray Associates on 01895 639 912.

118

NORTHCOTE ROAD, SW11

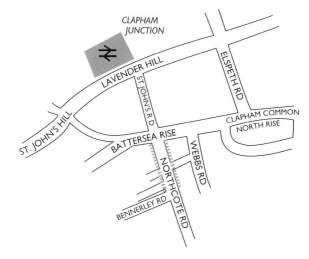

North end of Northcote Road.
BR: *Clapham Junction (Victoria, Waterloo)*
Buses: *35, 156, 170, 219, 295, C3 (Clapham Junction);*
319, G1, 239, 337 (Northcote Road)
Open: *Monday-Saturday 9am-5pm, Wednesday 9am-1pm*

Over the last decade a tide of demographic change has obviously
swept along Northcote Road. What was once an ordinary market
street is now a bustling strip of slick shops and eateries which are
very much a focus for SW11's smart set. Sadly, newer residents'
fondness for cappuccino froth, ciabatta rolls and designer knick-
knacks has meant demand for more traditional produce and services
has declined, with the result that what was once one of South West
London's busiest street markets has now all but disappeared. In fact,
you'd be hard pressed to call it a market at all: only a handful of

119

stalls are clinging onto trade, sadly strung out along a long line of empty pitch markings which underline the extent of what Northcote Road has lost.

Fruit and veg forms the core of what it is left with three stalls and an open shop unit offering a mixture of both traditional and more fancy produce, along with one which stocks fresh food with an Afro-Caribbean slant. Presentation and prices reflect the direction of the area's shops: few genuine bargains are to be had on stalls forced to match the tone of the street's many designer food outlets. That said, the stall holders are doing their best to dole out a bit of charisma and everything on sale looks pretty good quality, so it's not too hard to part with a few extra pence for your butternut squash or bag of mangoes. Similarly, two flower and plants stalls stock impressive displays of elegant blooms for discerning buyers.

If you do fancy a wade through Northcote Road's terracotta pots, aromatherapy products, gleaming kitchenware and farmhouse cheeses (and the range of upmarket goods on offer is certainly pretty tempting for those who fancy a bit of lifestyle enhancement), then also have a look in the street's charity shops. Perhaps due to the area's new found affluence, their stock of clothes and books are noticeably better than the norm, with some serious bargains crammed into a number of nicely cluttered outlets. You're spoilt for choice on the beverage front in Northcote Road with a café about every ten paces, but for the greasy spoon traditionalist, the Northcote Café at No. 74 is a croissant-free zone which does cheap breakfasts and lunches.

Getting a Stall

For further details contact Wandsworth Council (see appendix).

NORTH END ROAD, SW6

Along the east side of North End Road,
from Walham Grove to Lillie Road.
Tube: *Fulham Broadway (District)*
Buses: *28, 391 (North End Road); 74, 190 (Lillie Road);*
C4, 11, 14, 211, 295 (Fulham Broadway)
Open: *(Main market) Monday-Saturday 7am-5/6pm, Thursday 7am-*
1/2pm (Saturday busiest day);
(Crowthers Market) @ 282 North End Road (opp. Anselm Road)
Monday, Wednesday-Saturday 10.30am-5pm; Sunday 11am-4.30pm

Although SW6 has a smart reputation, the area north west of
Fulham Broadway forms a rectangle of pretty ordinary streets,
slotted in amongst other, posher districts. The North End Road
reflects the contrast, starting off relatively classy but becoming more
and more scruffy as you walk northwards past bomb-damaged
architecture and a string of £1 shops and cheap chainstores.
With its steady weekday flow of shoppers and Saturday bottlenecks
(when the range of stalls is far wider), North End Road's market is

obviously well used. It services mainly everyday needs with an extensive array of goods from fruit and veg to carpets and pet-care accessories with the odd ultra-specialist stall selling Hoover bags or deli-style cheeses and pâtés. The flower shop and stall on the corner of Walham Grove has a wide, well-priced selection, and the bedding and household stalls further up the road do a good deal on basics like bath towels and frying pans; the fish stalls also have reasonably-priced and sometimes fairly adventurous things on offer. At the very top end of the market, the perfume and cosmetics stall also knows how to pull in the punters, with false nails, nail varnish, lipsticks etc. all going for wholesale prices (from 50p), along with "copy" perfumes, which at £2.50 are well worth it for the names alone: "Obvious" (Obsession), "Elope" (Escape), and "Passive" (Passion).

The fruit and veg stalls form the largest contingent and attract the most customers, with a lot of casual as well as regular shoppers hooked in by impressive bargains, like 12 kiwi fruits for £1 and 3 pineapples for £1.20. The core range of fairly conserva-tive ingredients (although Mediterranean vegetables, and the occa-sional exotic fruit are dotted about) and old-fashioned displays: regi-ments of pears and apples sitting pertly on pink tissue paper – help conjure visions of Irish stew and crusted fruit pies. If you need a breather, the best place is the Valley Restaurant (at the north end of the market), which dishes up Lebanese specialities as well as normal burger bar fare. North End Road also has a serviceable donut café, a chip shop and a bakery that offers cheap baklava, while Vanston Place has two Italian stop-offs: Alimentari, a serious deli/café, and Mario's, a greasy spoon with net-curtained homeliness.

Crowther's Market

Situated half-way up the market on the west side of the street, this now well-established "indoor" market is an oasis of cluttered idiosyncrasy and a welcome break in the strip of bland retail outlets into which it seems to have crash-landed. Housed in a slightly dog-eared but still elegant candy-blue Georgian mansion house, and sprawling Tardis-like into a courtyard and stable block behind, Crowther's Market is in itself a good reason to make a trip to the North End Road.

In the courtyard and outbuildings, and spread over the floors of the main house, a tide of refreshingly well-priced junk, furniture, serious antiques, second-hand bikes, thirties-to-seventies clothes, jewellery, bric-à-brac and kitchenware washes up some quirky bargains – nearly all of which undercut the retro-chic price tags of West End second-hand shops. The strange mix of architecture at the back (the colonnade was stripped from a site in the city in Victorian times) gives the courtyard a film-set feel, with chairs, tables, crock-ery and garden statues spilling out higgledy-piggledy into the open air. In the stables, house clearance fare may throw up the odd find, and in the left-hand corner as you go in, a small unit sells inexpen-sive pieces of classic sixties and seventies furniture.

At the very top of the main house there is also a good food stop: The Gallery Café does baked spuds, pasta, soup and sandwiches and Sunday lunch for £3.50, with newspapers, framed pictures and tablecloths making for a homely atmosphere. Other units include an aromatherapy shop and The Seedbank, which apparently is the base for a Europe-wide trade in marijuana seeds – all above board, as it's only illegal to germinate them.

Getting a stall

For further details about a stall at Northcote Road Market contact Hammersmith & Fulham Council (see appendix). For stalls in Crowthers Market call 020 7385 8481.

PETTICOAT LANE, E1

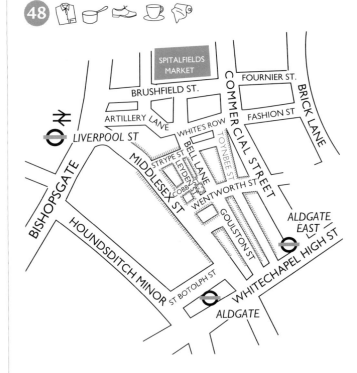

Middlesex Street and Wentworth Street, and adjacent streets and lanes.

Tube: *Aldgate (Metropolitan, Circle),*
Aldgate East (District, Hammersmith & City),
Liverpool Street (Circle, Central, Hammersmith & City, Metropolitan)
BR: *Battersea Park*
Buses: *5, 42, 78, 100 (Houndsditch Minories)*
5, 8, 26, 35, 43, 47, 48, 78, 149, 242, 243A (Liverpool Station)
Open: *All streets Sunday 9am-2pm,*
Wentworth Street only Monday-Friday 10am-2.30pm
(shops, fruit and veg and a reduced amount of clothing and general stalls)

Petticoat Lane still likes to play on its reputation as London's most famous street market, but it has declined in recent years and is not as popular as nearby Spitalfields or Brick Lane markets. Some tourists must still make the effort though, as the top end of Middlesex Street is peppered with Union Jack merchandise.

Despite this, Petticoat Lane is still impressively big and busy – it's a market you can lose yourself in. On a Sunday, the tides of people there to buy a cheap outfit or to just soak up the atmosphere can slow progress down to a shuffle. The streets are lined with hundreds of stalls, concentrating mainly on new clothing, shoes and accessories. Just the amount of people selling shirts or ties is enough to send you into option paralysis. Piles of cheap, cellophaned cotton, acrylic and silk seem to be the product of some mass breeding programme, as at each turn more cut-price bargains block your path. Classic price-busting multipacks of knickers, socks and boxer shorts are everywhere, and massive volumes of ladies dresses and separates are also available. Although there's not much outside the purely functional or bandwagon fashion spectrums, some of the "exclusive" name selections (like "Denial" or "Cute of London") of wholesale skirts, trousers and tops offer the odd pleasingly silly-frilly item for a fiver and some of the shoes are quite groovy for under a tenner. Some of the sports stores on Wentworth Street also feature a few bargains on brand-name trainers.

Retail-throwback stores like Benny Dees (Middlesex Street) stock good cheap bras (around a fiver) and ranges of staples like plain T-shirts and leggings. Petticoat Lane is also particularly good for leather belts (a decent one will only set you back £10), bags and luggage. And if you're fairly decisive, a visit to the "Designer Market" between Middlesex and Goulston Streets could save you serious money on leather jackets and coats. There must be literally hundreds of different styles hung up on the walls, and the amount of different traders with similar stock means productive haggling is an option. The other wholesale shops like "Cockney Touch" don't do much to broaden the range of desirable buys, appearing to concentrate mainly on the ritzy 'n' glitzy senior lady shopper. But even though it's no high-fashion paradise, Petticoat Lane is normally pretty lively, with traders ready to give out a bit of back-chat or

Petticoat Lane

advice: "Great fit those trousers! Nice and tight on the bum!"– to customers game for a bit of banter.

Stand-out specialisms at Petticoat Lane include the international textile shops, which sell everything from African wax prints to Indian sari fabric. At prices ranging from around £10 for four yards you can easily afford to do some fairly dramatic home-swagging or make yourself a sumptuous wrap-fabric dress or skirt. The top end of the market is also a magnet for "demonstrators" – the people whose job it is to flog us the fragile hope that our lives will be better if we can shred, shine or sharpen something five seconds quicker. Few can resist the power of the patter. Mr Euro-Tool, Mr Shine-Wipe or Mr Borner V-Slicer are performers in the old tradition, so watch, admire and learn. The evangelists at the Bishopsgate end of Middlesex Street might not have such funky props, but the sales message is just as heartfelt: their energetic sing-songs are now a market staple on a Sunday.

Petticoat Lane Market extends down a number of streets, so there are plenty of places to eat as you go round. At the top end of Middlesex Street, City Corner does classic greasy dishes with the odd bit of ciabatta thrown in, Happy Days on Goulston Street and John & Steve's Plaice on Toynbee Street offer chips-with-everything style lunches, and Falafel King on Wentworth Street and The Ciabatta Shop on the corner of Middlesex Street and New Goulston Street dish up slightly less leaden options. Vernasca's on Wentworth Street is a period-piece banquette and wood panel classic, serving a variety of solid lunches with charm as a mandatory side order. For something a bit more sophisticated, try the Barcelona Tapas Bar (not open on a Sunday) or the shellfish stall (the plump king prawns in garlic and butter smell fantastic) on Middlesex Street. Those wanting to make their trip to the market cholestrol-lite, can stock up on fruit and veg from the stalls on Wentworth Street.

Getting a Stall
The council are trying to vary the range of the market and are therefore discouraging any more clothing stalls. For further details contact Tower Hamlets Central Market Office (see appendix).

PICCADILLY MARKET, W1

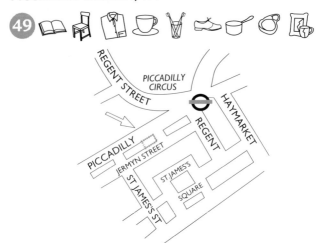

St James' Church Yard, Piccadilly.
Tube: *Piccadilly Circus (Piccadilly, Bakerloo),*
Green Park (Victoria, Jubilee, Piccadilly)
Buses: *38, 22, 19, 14, 9, 8*
Open: *Tuesday 10am-6pm (Antiques),*
Wednesday-Saturday 10am-6pm (Arts and Crafts)

Piccadilly Market is an oasis of tranquillity compared to the traffic
and crowds of Piccadilly. The heavy flagstone paving and large
gates of St James' Church courtyard give this market a unique and
peaceful atmosphere, there are ancient trees which provide shade in
the summer and benches for you to sit and relax. Between
Wednesday and Saturday the market concentrates on arts and
crafts, with about 25 stalls selling crafts from around the world such
as African Ashanti masks for £30, Kenyan chess sets for £60,
brooches for between £3 and £6, and modern prints of London
for £25. The new watches were good value with funky Baby
Shock look-a-likes for only £10, as were the chunky Aran-style
jumpers for a mere £29.95.

Piccadilly Market

The market is particularly interesting on a Tuesday when it concentrates on antiques, collectables and bric-à-brac. What's particularly good about the market is the varied range of goods and prices on offer. One stall has extravagant fifties Italian glassware for between £25 and a modest £4 and a very grand set of silverware which the trader lamented he had not been able to sell despite dropping the price to £70. The stall specialising in purses carries an equally varied stock with a simple silver purse for only £3 alongside an authentic thirties art deco purse for £49. Well worth a browse, the watch and knick-knack stall sells items like a forties men's watch for £40 and more expensive items like a Rolex for £2,000 (kept safe in a glass case). The stall specialising in magnifying glasses, prints and pens has a good display and welcomes those who want to give the pens a try before making up their minds. Not all the stalls are traditional in nature, one has a display of Beatles memorabilia, including an Abbey Road commemorative plate for £25, another specialises in all things Russian. Other stalls offer jewellery, books and vintage clothes.

In terms of refreshment the old Wren Café has been replaced by one of the ubiquitous Aroma Cafés in the wing of the church, which serves prepared snacks and a very good cappuchino and also has plenty of outdoor seating for when the weather is fine.

Getting a Stall

If you are interested in having a stall at Piccadilly Market contact the rector's office on 020 7734 4511 or visit the rectory (in the court yard of the church) during market hours.

PORTOBELLO, W11

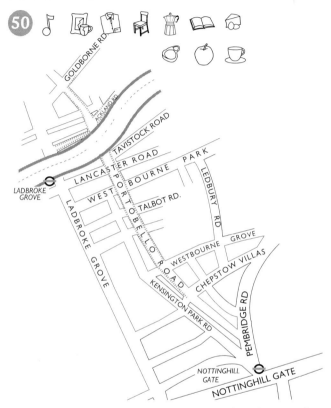

Portobello Road from (and including) Goldborne Road to Chepstow Villas.
Tube: *Notting Hill Gate (Central, District, Circle),*
Ladbroke Grove (Metropolitan)
Buses: *12, 70, 94 (Notting Hill Gate); 31, 28, 31 (Pembridge Road);*
70, 7 (Westbourne Park Road); 7, 23, 52, 70 (Ladbroke Grove)
Open: *Saturday 8am-5.30pm (Antiques), Monday-Saturday 9am-5pm*
(General Market), Sunday 9am-1pm (Car Boot Sale)

".., the best and oddest market for antiques in London..." V.S.Pritchett

131

Portobello is very difficult to describe as, like Camden Market, it varies from day to day and is made up of several markets in one. If you want to see the market in full swing the best day to visit is Saturday when the whole market is open and Portobello Road is packed with visitors from around the world. In the space of a few metres you can here Spanish, French, German, Japanese and of course English (although in many cases spoken with an American accent).

Portobello can be very roughly divided into three part: the antiques section at the south end of the street (nearest to Nottting Hill Gate tube), the general fruit and veg and new clothes market which is in the central part of the market and finally the second-hand, junk and fashion part of the market which begins at the Westway and extends onto Goldborne Road. If you're not inter-ested in antiques and want to visit the north end of the market it's a good idea to approach it from Ladbroke Grove tube or take one of the back streets because simply walking the length of Portobello Road from Notting Hill Gate is exhausting when the market is in full swing. If you have an aversion to crowds the Sunday Car Boot sale under the Westway is a more relaxing alternative and of course during the week Portobello Road between Lonsdale Road and Lancaster Road is the site of a very fine fruit and veg market.

Chepstow Villas to Lonsdale Road
(Antiques and Collectables)

This part of Portobello Road is so quiet on weekdays that visitors to the numerous antique shops in the area are often suspected of being spies for rival dealers, as V.S. Pritchett describes in *London Perceived*. This all changes on Saturdays when the shops expand onto the street, other itinerant traders arrive in the early hours and the street gives itself over to the hordes of visitors arriving from the direction of Notting Hill tube station. The market starts from the junction with Chepstow Villas and it is here that you will often encounter your first busker of the day, on one visit a string quartet were doing their best to master Vivaldi despite the winter cold numbing their fingers. Although this part of the market is the first stop for eager tourists and prices tend to be high, there are still some good buys to be found. A complete fifties tea service in black china with a gold edging was good value at £85, as were the paper-weights for £6.

Further north is Denbigh Terrace which is host to several stalls including the long established camera stall with all sorts of unusual items such as a sixties Yushika twin-lens camera for £55. Just opposite Denbigh Close is Chelsea Galleries, from where several dealers do business and which has the added advantage of having a café upstairs. The junction with Westbourne Grove has a lot to offer with The Good Fairy indoor antiques market (Stall Enquiries 01634 233 900) to the right, just behind one of Portobello's best pubs, The Earl of Lonsdale. Outside the pub a few stalls sell modern goods such as chunky jumpers, cheap CD's and gifts like inflatable chairs for only £6. On the opposite side of the junction is the Antiques Gallery indoor market (stall enquiries 020 7747 5240), and stalls extend west along Westbourne Grove, offering anything from bric-à-brac to fine antiques. It is here that you'll find The Tea Room, which serves traditional cream teas. For those who like charity shops, there's a very good Oxfam shop two minutes walk from here east along Westbourne Grove.

Continuing north along Portobello Road there are some of the most established stalls selling anything from toy soldiers to antique telescopes. It is here that I found a wonderful thirties gold-framed oil painting for £250. If this is a little beyond your budget, you can always seek comfort from a cappuccino and pastry from the stall situated just past Vernon Yard. The Admiral Vernon Antiques Market (stall enquiries 020 7727 5242), one of Portbello's oldest indoor markets, is also located here. Lonsdale Road marks the begining of the end for the antiques part of the market, although a few antique stalls continue after it, including one specialising in colourful glassware from the fifites to the seventies.

Lonsdale Road to Lancaster Road
(Food, Flowers and Clothing)

Between Lonsdale Road and Elgin Crescent the first modern cloth-ing stalls appear, the best being the jumper and tops stall on the junction with Colville Terrace which sells excellent polo neck jumpers for only £13. If you're looking for a leather jacket then the stall on Elgin Crescent sells good quality fashionable jackets for between £60 and £120.

Further north the market becomes more food-orientated with excellent fruit and veg stalls, a stall selling dried fruit, nuts, herbs and spices and the welcome addition of a fine bread and patisserie stall. The air is fragrant with the aroma of cooking meat from the German wurst stall, and there's a café and pub on the street if you're ready for a sit down. The coffee and tea stall that used to roast beans on Blenheim Crescent has gone all respectable and opened The Tea and Coffee Plant on Portobello Road. If, surrounded by all these wonderful ingredients, you are short of a few ideas as to what to do with them, don't forget Books for Cooks on Blenheim Crescent. Between Blenheim Crescent and Westbourne Park Road there are many more fruit and veg stalls offering anything from the humble tomato to Purslane and oyster mushrooms. Complementing the stalls is an excellent fresh fish shop and, although, sadly, the Applewood Farm Shop has closed down, it's at least been replaced by the very good Retro Clothing Shop. In this part Portobello Road there are plenty of places to eat, among them the Daytime Café Night Time Tandoori, Café Bellini, the very trendy Ground Floor Bar and the Warwick Castle pub at the junction with Westbourne Park Road.

Between Westbourne Park Road and Lancaster Road there are some excellent food stalls including G. Piper & Son, the long-established fresh fish stall, a poultry stall and a deli stall selling things like feta cheese and olives. For those in search of flora to look at rather than eat, there's also a flower stall offering some very good deals including 3 bunches of daffs for £1. If you need a rest before embarking on the next phase of your shopping trip, don't forget Eve's Market Café which is good for basic English grub.

Portobello

Lancaster Road to the Westway
(New Clothing and Household Goods)
At this point Portobello Market slightly loses the plot, with the stalls drifting between cheap watches and bags and a few reasonably-priced fabric stalls. Among the best stalls here is the one selling cheap trainers – all of them copies of well-known brands. At Tavistock Road there's a large square and it's here that buskers perform during the summer. There are also two very good cafés in this square: a mediterranean cafe, Il Girasole, and the Vegetarian Café. If you prefer your refreshment to be served in a loud and trendy environment there's also the Beatbar at 265 Portobello Road.

Under the Westway and west up to Ladbroke Grove
(Retro and new clothing, CD's and Records, Books and Collectables)
The huge concrete flyover known as the Westway is a landmark on Portobello Road and also offers cover beneath its arches for new street clothing stalls as well as a small square of stalls specialising in collectables, jewellery and a good many seventies table lamps. The Westway also shelters some of Portobello's best eateries including Pitta the Great (bad pun, good food), Makan Malasian café and the Sausage & Mash Café. To the left, within the concrete structure is a small arcade crammed with shops selling anything from designer clothes, to jewellery and good value bedding.

Just north of the Westway are two interconnected canopies that house hundreds of stalls selling new designer clothes, retro clothing from the forties to the seventies, funky designer bags and modern jewellery. The diversity of clothing sold here is reflected in the different music being played, from reggae to jungle. There are also one or two unusual stalls which are fun to look at, like the one selling designer cannabis rolling trays for those that have turned a habit into a hobby.

One of the areas of Portobello Market which has really expanded is the pedestrian walkway that runs west, parallel to the Westway. Four years ago it did not extend much beyond the canopies, but it now has stalls all the way to Ladbroke Grove offering all kinds of music, clothing, jewellery and a solitary lock-up selling junk and even a second-hand book stall. If you want refreshment there are several good food stalls selling Indian and Jamaican

food and an internet café, Dot Com, which affords a great view of
the market from its balcony.

To the east of Portobello Road and also running parallel to
the Westway, Acklam Road is a mecca for those who enjoy second-
hand and junk shopping. There's a more chaotic feel to this part of
the market as old guitars are displayed alongside vacuum cleaners
and old books. There are always bargains to found here, but you
might have to search to find them. The four seventies orange plastic
and chrome kitchen chairs were not difficult to spot and were an
excellent buy for £45. There's a good deal of bargain hi-fi equipment to be found here, such as a Technics tape deck for £25, but
it's always a risk buying such things from a junk stall. If all this
bargain hunting makes you hungry, try Falafel King on the corner
of Portobello Road and Acklam Road which as its name suggests,
does great falafel.

Portobello Road from Acklam Road to Golborne Road
*(Retro and new clothing, bric-à-brac, furniture, household and
electrical goods)*
This is one of the best parts of the market if you enjoy bargain
hunting and don't mind sifting through a lot of junk to find something special. You can usually tell the pricing policy of the stall by
the way things are displayed, the better organised stalls with a selection of well chosen clothes are more expensive than those selling
clothes in piles like a jumble sale, usually for 50p an item. If you
want to acquire retro chic without the effort of hunting for it, there
are several very good classic clothing shops in this part of
Portobello (Start at Orsini, Johnsons and The Antique Clothing
Shop). There's also a smattering of new clothing stalls at this end of
the market selling trendy streetwear often at a lower price than
similar stalls further south on Portobello Road. This is also a good
place to find old furniture and bric-à-brac for the home with
several interesting stalls and two long-established shops: Portobello
307 and a shop with no visible name just off Portobello Road on
Oxford Gardens – both of which spread their wares onto the pavement to attract passing trade. The independent cafés in this part of
the market have all changed hands and gone up-market, leaving you
a choice between Ruby in the Dust, Asian Cuisine Restaurant and
the Japanese Canteen for sustenance.

Further north along Portobello Road there are even more junk and bric-à-brac stalls with some traders simply laying their stock on the side of the road. It is here that some genuine bargains can be found, such as the men's Reiss designer trousers recently picked up here for only £3. As well as the junk, there are a few trendy new clothes stalls and several selling household goods and one specialising in new end-of-range discounted hi-fi, TV and video equipment, and another offering any three CD's for £10. If you're feeling parched after all the bargain hunting you could try The Carnarvon pub at the junction with Golborne Road.

Golborne Road from Portobello Road to St Ervans Road
(Junk, furniture, and fruit and veg)
Although just around the corner from Portobello Road, this part of the market has a more local feel with few tourists venturing this far. It's well worth making the effort as there are some excellent junk stalls and shops dealing in second-hand furniture, and one, on the junction with Warnington Road, selling more distinctive retro furniture and architectural salvage items. Among the bargains was a very fine Victorian style set of bath taps with shower attachment for only £40 (usually over £150 new). The cultural mix is also different on the Goldborne Road with many Portuguese and Moroccans living in the area, hence the numerous shops and cafés catering for those communities. The north side of the road has a few good fruit and veg stalls, but with none of the junk or bric-à-brac found on the south side, but it's a great place to find unusual Middle Eastern cooking ingredients. Among the places to eat and drink in this area are the Moroccan Café, Oporto, Lisboa Patisserie and the Havana Café. If you want more basic British food try the Golborne Café on the north side of the street.

Getting a Stall
There are two bodies responsible for running market stalls in Portobello:
a. Most of the market is run by Kensington & Chelsea Council (see Appendix).
b. Country Wide operate the stalls under the canopy and along the Westway, for further details phone 01562 777 877.

QUEEN'S CRESCENT, NW5

Queen's Crescent, between Malden Road and Grafton Road.
Tube: *Kentish Town or Chalk Farm (Northern Line)*
Buses: *31, 168, 24, 27, 31, 168 (Chalk Farm Road)*
Open: *Thursday 8.30am-2.30pm and*
Saturday (busiest day) 8.30am-4pm.

Tucked into a tangle of residential streets, Queen's Crescent is very much a community market. The atmosphere makes up for the slightly dreary location, with people swapping gossip and news in chatty clumps down the length of the street. Stall holders generally have a no-frills approach, with a lot of goods piled in open crates, or propped on boxes, but are friendly enough to indulge a bit of pottering. Rival fruit and veg stalls mean some healthy bargains, and stockpiled bras, socks and undies all go for around a pound, while the plant stall has sophisticated greenery for under a tenner. Although unexciting, the other stalls are worth a look for good deals on new clothes, trainers, fish, meat, flowers, bedlinen, cheap groceries, electrical goods, ethnic bric-à-brac, kitchen equipment, jewellery and stationery. A couple of shambolic junk stalls also spill out of lock-ups and shops: the odd nice plate, glass or cup can be found for around 50p.

There are a few places to eat along the Crescent, but best are Bull's Bagels, the Blue Sea Fish Shop and the Gossip Stop Café which, with its lemon yellow walls, cheap fry-ups and Jam Roly Poly (£1), is a cheery place to work on the waistline. At the Malden Road junction, the pet shop and adjacent junk and furniture shop, Charlie Gimberts, are worth a look. The Kentish Town City Farm is also nearby in Cressfield Close for a temporary escape from city streets.

Getting a stall
For further details contact Camden Council (see appendix).

QUEEN'S MARKET, E13

South of Upton Park Station, next to Queen's Road
Tube: Upton Park (Metropolitan, District)
Buses: 58, 104, 330
Open: Monday-Saturday 9am-5pm, Wednesday 9am-12.30pm

Queen's Market has a long history dating back to Victoria's reign but in the sixties the market was moved to this purpose-built square and in 1979 a low roof was built over it. Twenty years later the place looks squalid and run-down, with little light penetrating beyond the entrance. Despite these badly-planned changes to the market, it is still thriving and even on a wet Monday morning crowds mill around the hundred or so stalls in search of bargains.

One of the reasons this market is still doing well is the large Asian and African communities in Upton Park who still prefer the hustle and bustle of a market to the antiseptic atmosphere of a supermarket. The market is good value for fruit and veg with lots of stalls competing for your custom and bargains like 4 avocados for £1 and bananas for only 15p per lb as well as 5lbs of Desirée potatoes for only 75p. Queen's is also a great place to find all kinds of Asian and African produce, with many specialist food outlets offering things like Dasheen leaves and bunches of fresh Pachoy. The handful of fresh fish stalls carry a varied range of catches and are good value with smoked haddock for only £1.49 lb alongside more exotic things like conger eel and octopus. The market also has a profusion of butchers offering all manner of bloody bargains as well as a stall selling farm-fresh eggs.

Queen's Market is also the place for cheap fabric with lots of stalls offering colourful and plain material (including African and Asian designs) with prices starting from £1 per metre. If sewing isn't your thing, there are stalls selling cheap and cheerful clothing, including one specialising in bargain footwear and even one sellng tacky plastic watches for only £5.99. Although many of the consumer durables here are of limited appeal, the stall offering large stainless steel pans for £16 is excellent value, as is the discount underwear stall located at the front of the market.

For such a large and busy market, Queen's is poorly served for cafés and restaurants. If you do want refreshment, all the eating places are located at the front of the market on Green Street and include Crisp and Crusty Bakers, Queen's Fish Bar and a little further down the road – the other side of Upton Park tube station – Duncan's Pie, Mash and Eel shop.

Getting a Stall
For further details contact Newham Council (see appendix).

RIDLEY ROAD, E8

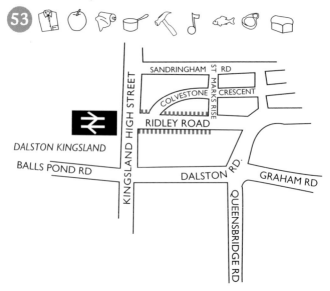

Ridley Road, between Kingsland High Street and St Mark's Rise.
BR: *Dalston Kingsland (North London Line),*
Hackney Downs (Liverpool Street)
Buses*: 67, 149, 242, 243, 243A (Kingsland High Street);*
236 (St Mark's Rise)
Open*: Monday-Saturday 9am-5pm*

Ridley Road is one of North London's biggest markets, with the attitude to match. Running the length of a curvaceous street of lock-up shop units joining the main road next to the Kingsland Shopping Centre, this market is the place where locals from Dalston's diverse communities come and stock up on cheap food and essentials – even on a weekday it's buzzing. The Afro-Caribbean influence in both Dalston and its market is particularly strong, and not only in terms of the massive selection of unusual food products. As the streams of people increase towards midday, the lively – and occasionally slightly abrasive – atmosphere is stoked by shops blasting out reggae and groups of traders and shoppers stopping mid-flow to shoot the breeze.

Although Ridley Road is by no means just a food market, the massive selection of both fresh and preserved produce is probably the magnet drawing most shoppers. Further down towards St Mark's Rise goods become increasingly alien, with tropical standards like mango, cassava and sweet potato joined by baskets and trestles piled with unfamiliar leaves, vegetables, meat and fish, and lurid drinks like "Sky Juice" on sale by the glass – everyday London seems swallowed up in an atmosphere grafted straight from the Caribbean. The sheer number of rival stalls and shops means you are spoilt for bargains: with each trader offering something at a discount price (like 4 star fruit for £1) you can stock up for a specialist meal for well under a tenner. Staples like lentils, oil, nuts and flour are also extremely cheap, although quantities tend to be large.

In addition, the large local Turkish community means that there are plenty of Mediterranean-style vegetables on offer, with good prices on key ingredients like lemons (14 for £1), coriander (40p for a huge bunch) and mixed peppers (6 for a £1). More conventional produce is also well stocked, with prices like 80p for a Gala melon, 40p for a large clump of watercress and 30 eggs for £3 standard in rows of competing stalls. The only drawback with Ridley Road is that it can get very busy, with the narrow gap between stalls clogged with people trying to move in every direction at once. When this happens, traders get a bit shirty if you're not buying courgettes for ten, and might talk you into buying more than you want. Stand firm if you just want a pound of spuds. (A warning to the squeamish: Ridley Road is peppered with stalls selling meat and fish products which bear little resemblance to the vacuum-packed portions in Tescos: turkey gizzards, saltfish, goat stomachs, cows and pigs feet are all piled up, picked over and chopped up in full view.)

Food is definitely the thing at Ridley Road, but there are plenty of other goods on offer, with standard market clobber (electrical, cheap and brand-name clothes and shoes, bedding, underwear, cosmetics and hair accessories) dotted throughout, and a good batch of textile units

Ridley Road

and stalls selling haberdashery and vivid materials like African wax prints (6 yards for £30), sequinned voiles and rainbow selections of satin, cotton and acrylic mixes. For a break, Len's Café (half-way down on the left) is secreted underneath the lock-ups for an almost subterranean cup of tea, and there are a host of take-away stalls selling Turkish and Indian snacks; and the Ridley Bagel Bakery is another cheap way of plugging a hole. At 41 Kingsland High Street, Shanghai serves dim sum throughout the day in a listed interior that used to belong to the area's famous pie and mash shop. If you're not too laden with groceries, round the corner in Ashwin Street (off Dalston Lane), there is a big house clearance furniture warehouse which looks like a good bet for finding retro classics in amongst yesterday's clunky oak and pine mediocrities.

Getting a Stall

For further details contact Hackney Council (see appendix).

ROMAN ROAD, E3

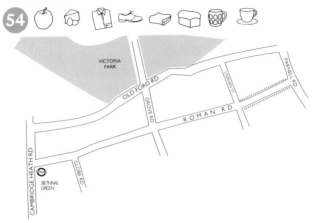

Roman Road from St Stephen's Road to Parnell Road.
Tube: *Mile End (Central, Metropolitan and District)*
Buses: *8, D6 (Roman Road); 277, 333 (Grove Road)*
Open: *Tuesday, Thursday and Saturday 8.30am-5.30pm*

Roman Road and its market are a strange mix of the cosmopolitan and the parochial. Approaching the market along Roman Road you will pass a photography gallery, an art gallery, several smart designer clothes shops and even a Buddhist Centre, and yet by the time you reach the market it feels as though you are in the heart of the East End. Most of the people that visit the market are locals and one of the stall holders spoke of the other side of Victoria Park as though it were some distant and exotic land. Although the market conforms to many of the stereotypes of the East End it is actually a lot cleaner and smarter than commonly assumed and with Victoria Park and the Regent Canal nearby, a place well worth visiting.

The market begins at the junction with St Stephen's Road and here you'll find a small privately-run indoor market, which is currently being redeveloped and so it only has a couple of stalls selling clothes and a few pieces of Italian furniture. One of the first stalls in the market proper, is one selling good quality fabric for as little as £1.99 per yard (the metric system has not yet been adopted here). Another stall sells cheap women's clothes, revealing one garment at a time from a box. It might sound strange but the stall is always crowded with women jostling for bargains, so it must work.

Further along there's a stall selling fashionable shoes at around £20 a pair and another dealing in cheap fashion clothing with most items for less than £10. I found a trendy bodywarmer here for £15, which was selling for between £20 and £25 at Portobello. There's also a very good sweets stall if you fancy a treat, and on the corner of Galdstone Place is the DAWN charity shop which is worth a browse. There are two indoor markets around this part of the market. The first, Jubilee Shopping Hall, is rather dilapidated and largely empty, but the second, Harman Indoor Shopping Centre, is still busy with stalls selling clothes and shoes, jewellery and a popular café. It is at this point in the market, between Libra Road and Hewison Street, that most of the fruit and veg stalls are located. The fruit and veg are of good quality but, unlike somewhere like Ridley Road, there is not much of a cultural mix here, and the food is not very varied as a result.

The eastern end of the market is the most interesting for discounted clothing with several stalls specialising in slight seconds and end of line garments from leading designers and high street chains. It is here that I discovered a wonderful French Connection t-shirt for only £5 and a pair of Next trousers for only £3. The stall selling underwear is also good value, but its a good idea to stick to white material, as the cheaper coloured stuff tends to run.

If you're feeling peckish after your trek (Roman Road is one of London's longest markets) there are several good places to get refreshment, among them L. Randolfi, the Bagel Bakery for basic grub, and G. Kelly if you want to try a traditional pie and eel shop.

Getting a Stall

Most of the market is run by Tower Hamlets Council (see appendix). The indoor parts of the market are managed by Sherman Waterman Associates Ltd who can be contacted on 020 7240 7405.

Roman Road

SHEPHERD'S BUSH, W12

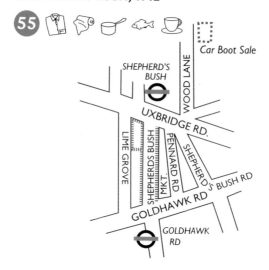

Shepherd's Bush Market,
between Uxbridge Road and Goldhawk Road W12
Tube: *Shepherd's Bush, Goldhawk Road (Metropolitan Line)*
Buses: *49, 95, 207, 237, 260, 607, 283 (Uxbridge Road)*
Open: *Monday-Saturday 9am-5pm, Thursday 9am-1pm*

Shepherd's Bush is a remarkably mixed area. On Shepherd's Bush
Green there are large pubs packed with young people drinking too
much beer and watching sport while just down Goldhawk Road at
the entrance to Shepherd's Bush Market, Middle-Eastern women in
full Islamic dress await the arrival of their limousines to take them
home. It struck me as strange that women shopping at the local
market should have a limousine, but it emerged that the limos are
in fact glorified taxis that turn up every ten minutes to pick up
their fares.

Entering the market from Goldhawk Road it is evident that
the cultural mix is even more complex with many African, Middle-
Eastern, West Indian and Asian people living, shopping and trading
in the area. The market also has a variety of outlets with shops,
lock-ups and stalls all vying for your attention as they extend paral-

lel to the overhead Metropolitan line with the occasional sight of a tube train to remind you that this is still London and not some foreign bazaar.

The market does not just run along the eastern side of the tube line, but has a fairly large square and passageway on the western side which connects to the main market via two narrow arches. It is in this smaller maze of shops that most of the specialist African food stalls are situated as well as a few selling African music along with the usual mix of street fashion, cheap shoes, bags and the excellent Tahanie's which sells fabric by the yard. Among some of the more interesting outlets is the shop selling reconditioned TV's and VCR's and the excellent Footsie 101 which offers fashionable footwear at below high street prices.

The market is especially strong on fresh food, with many top-notch fruit and veg stalls ranging from those dealing in standard fare to others with more exotic produce. One such stall is located about half way down the market and has all kinds of unusual vegetables – yams, cassava, plantain and dry pumpkin. One of the traders here managed to combine work and pleasure as he flirted outrageously with his female customers. There are also several good butchers within the market selling basics as well as more recherché things to cater for the African community such as pigs trotters and cows tongues. Likewise there are plenty of good fresh fish stalls offering anything from smoked haddock to fresh tuna and red snapper.

Although many of the things found at Shepherd's Bush Market are unexceptional, the atmosphere and diversity of the place make it worth visiting. If you go on a Saturday try and make it to the car boot sale which is just 5 minutes walk from here (in the car park on Wood Lane). The market also has some of the best fast food stalls in the capital to keep you going on your trek. There are several stalls that serve delicious falafel in pitta bread and, for Indian food, Babujee's stall in the square to the west of the tube line is fantastic. If your tastes are a little more conservative, several stalls serve British grub and, for traditionalists, there is always A. Cooke pie and mash shop on Goldhawk Road.

Getting a Stall

The market is run by London Transport and there are all kinds of sites available, for more details phone 020 7918 3097.

SMITHFIELD, EC1

Charterhouse Street
Tube: *Farringdon and Barbican*
(Circle, Metropolitan and Hammersmith and City)
Buses: *55, 243, 505 (Clerkenwell Road)*
Open: *Monday-Friday 4am-12noon*

Smithfield Market is the last wholesale market in London to remain on its original site and meat has been sold here for over eight hundred years. The present building is an impressive edifice of iron, stone and brick designed by Sir Horace Jones (who also designed Leadenhall Market) and built in 1866. Behind the immutable exterior, however, things have not stayed still and the market has undergone a £70 million redevelopment in recent years.

If you walk through the central archway at the bottom of St John Street and take a look down any of the buyers avenues the change is easy to see. The interior of the massive Victorian building has been stripped out and, instead of the rather dark chaotic workings of the old market, new avenues have been created with each trader selling meat from modern counters and the meat is unpacked behind glass screens direct from the lorries. These changes were primarily introduced to improve efficiency and conform to hygiene regulations, but they also make this a far more welcoming place for members of the public to shop, if also diminishing some of its spit and sawdust vitality.

Early in the morning all the trade is on a large commercial scale, with wholesalers, butchers and those buying for London's restaurants and hotels doing their business. After about eight in the morning trade begins to slow down and those interested in buying in smaller quantities can be more easily served. I asked one trader whether he could sell one of his corn-fed chickens, rather than the box of eight that cost £20. His response was friendly and succinct "oh yeah, we always welcome RM", and when he noticed my look of incomprehension he kindly explained "RM means ready money". There are some excellent meaty bargains to be found here making it a worthwhile destination if you have a large carnivorous family and a reasonable freezer compartment. Among the bargains were a large box of frozen chicken legs (about thirty legs) for £6.50, while more unusual things like prepared stewing rabbit were only £2.50 per box. Another change in favour of retail customers is the increase in prepared meats and other things like large pannetone cakes being sold here. Smithfield is a pleasant and friendly place to shop in the morning and there are usually a good few people strolling through the well-lit avenues looking for bargains.

There are lots of places to get refreshment in and around the market from early in the morning. Among the more established are The Hope and Sir Loin on St John Street (open from 6.30am) and the Fox & Anchor on Chamberhouse Street (open from 7am). Fields Sandwich Bar next door to The Hope does a great coffee and is open from 6.30am. There is also a Coffee Republic right on the corner of Cow Cross Street. Also on Cow Cross Street is an excellent veggie café called The Greenway, which is a welcome stop if you've had enough of meat for one morning.

SOUTH BANK BOOKMARKET, SE1

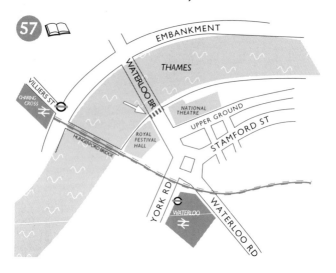

*Riverside Walk, under Waterloo Bridge
in front of the National Film Theatre, SE1.*
Tube/BR: *Waterloo (Northern and Piccadilly Line)*
Buses: *1, 4, 26, 68, 76, 168, 171, 176, 188,
341, 501, 505, 521, X68*
Open: *7 days a week 11am-7pm (till later in summer months)*

It would be hard to imagine a more perfect location for a book
market than on the south bank of the Thames, just outside the
National Film Theatre (NFT), under the protection of Waterloo
Bridge and with a fantastic view of the London skyline. Not only is
it a good place to browse for books but, with a broad tree-lined
pedestrian "boulevard", it also has a romantic atmosphere. I am not
alone in thinking this as, afterall, it was here that Hugh Grant made
his declaration of love in the film *Four Weddings and a Funeral* and I
know of at least one couple that carried out a good deal of their
courtship here. The secret of the place is that, although it is located
in the centre of London, it's spirit and atmosphere is reminiscent of

South Bank Bookmarket

the south bank of the Seine in Paris. After only a few minutes of browsing among the books I feel the urge to don a black polo neck, start smoking *Gitanes* and buy at least one book concerning existentialism.

The market has around one hundred tables heaving under the weight of thousands of books covering most subjects. Works by all the giants of European literature can be found here including such names as Dickens, Balzac, Henry James, Orwell, Steinbeck and Kafka. If you prefer a good page turner there are enough books by the likes of Jilly Cooper, Jeffery Archer and Catherine Cookson to keep you entertained. This is also a good market to visit for academic and reference books with plenty of philosophy, psychology, art history and architecture. Naturally, being in the heart of the South Bank Centre, London's only arts and culture complex (the centre offers cutting-edge art exhibitions at the Hayward Gallery, classical and contemporary concerts and dance performances at the Royal Festival and Queen Elizabeth Halls, repertory cinema and the annual London Film Festival at the NFT, plus a history of film at the Museum of the Moving Image), there is a good selection of plays, screenplays and books about film and theatre. Biographies are also well represented with anything from Kitty Kelly's prurient treatment of Frank Sinatra to more noble attempts to capture the lives of novelist Grahman Greene or movie star Greta Garbo. Likewise, there's a good mix of books on music with biographies of composers such as Haydn and Mozart alongside glossy picture books on the likes of Blur and the ubiquitous Spice Girls. There are also a fair few stalls selling mounted prints, usually illustrations taken from old books. The range of illustrations is fairly limited and a good deal of it consists of old maps, but there are sometimes things of interest to be uncovered, such as the collection of German graphic art dating from 1910 which could be bought here recently for £18 a print.

The South Bank Book Market is not the cheapest place to find second-hand books, with most paperbacks selling for around half their new price, but among the thousands of books on offer you can usually find the odd bargain such as the paperback edition of Pevsner's Outline of European Architecture I found recently for a mere £3. Anyway most of the people visiting here are really interested in enjoying the atmosphere and having a browse, rather than trying to save a few quid. If you fancy something to eat or drink after your intellectual exertions the NFT café is right next to the market, but the food is unexceptional and expensive. You might be better walking east along the embankment to Gabriel's Wharf which has lots of cafés and restaurants to choose from or visiting the Aroma coffee bar in the Royal Festival Hall.

Getting a Stall

There are only ten licenses to sell books on this site, and the current traders have no plans to leave. The waiting list for a license is now closed. In short you have more chance of winning the National Lottery than trading at this market.

SOUTHWARK PARK ROAD, SE16

Market Place off Southwark Park Road.
BR: *South Bermondsey*
Buses: *1, 199*
Open: *Monday-Saturday 9.30am-5pm*

Poor old Southwark Park Road. Stuck well below the Thames,
lined with squat sixties shoe-box shop units and sandwiched
between squalid estates and railway lines, the location doesn't
exactly scream hotspot. In the seventies the council made things
worse by giving the road over entirely to the relentless south-east-
wards bound traffic, side-lining its once-famous street market into a
bland precinct. Even now, despite the pretty ash trees and bright
municipal benches, the market's slightly artificial setting doesn't
seem to help pull in passing trade from the busy high street – the
Sainsburys at Surrey Quays is also leeching the market's customers.

But it's not all gloom and doom. Although in terms of its
range of goods the market isn't exceptional, there is still a bit of

atmosphere washing about and most traders seem to welcome banter with regulars. On offer is the normal mixture of things decorative, edible, readable or wearable (Saturdays bring out the most stalls): cheap men's clothes, sports gear, shoes and trainers; books (cowboys, wars, thrillers, and lurve), Victoriana prints, stationery, toys (the nostalgic can pick up a pea-shooter for 20p), carpets, nightwear and undies. But, as a local market, Southwark Park Road plays to its strengths, the best stalls being those piled high with cheaply priced fruit, veg, meat, eggs, cheese, fish, seafood and flowers.

The friendly fruit and veg man has plenty of regulars popping by for a pound of this or that, and with good reason. Although unremarkable in terms of the trendy or exotic, his produce includes some more uncommon indigenous varieties of fruit bowl mainstays, for example, on the apple front, Katys and Worcesters might also be available as an alternative to Discoveries or Granny Smiths. The plant and flower stall is excellent, with plenty of bright, cheap potted options like a sunflower plant for £2, a rubecia for just 80p or a candy-pink cyclamen for £1.20; the selection of bulbs is also quite impressive, and at just £1 for 10, tempting for those willing to invest some time in a bit of digging.

Southwark Park Road itself looks like a pretty unremarkable high street but a few of the shops offer some compelling bargains on household goods, so take a look if you've got time.

In case you're planning to stick around for a few hours, Southwark Park Road has its quota of cheap eateries. Avoid the soulless Star Grill in the market precinct and head instead for the Pop Inn Café, which dishes up special breakfasts for under £3 in a lively no-frills atmosphere.

Getting a Stall
For further details contact Southwark Council (see appendix).

SPITALFIELDS MARKET, E1

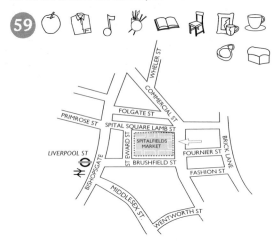

West side of Commercial Street between Folgate and Brushfield Street
Tube: *Liverpool Street (Central, Metro & Circle lines).*
Buses: *67 (Commercial Street);*
5, 8, 26, 35, 43, 47, 48, 78, 149, 242, 243A (Liverpool Station)
Car Parking: *Car park under the arches on Wheler Street 3 minutes walk from the market, charge £2.50.*
Open: *Monday-Friday 9am-6pm and weekends (food stalls and shops). Sunday 11am-3pm (Main Sunday Market).*

This huge Victorian building was home to one of London's largest wholesale fruit and veg markets, but in 1991 the business moved to a modern site in Hackney Wick and Spitalfields was transformed into an area for shops, cafés, sports facilities and, of course, the Sunday market.

The market had a rocky start in the early nineties when it specialised in organic fruit, veg and produce and many observers were sceptical about its future. Since those initial difficult years the market has diversified and, as a result, is now one of the major Sunday markets rivaling nearby Brick Lane and Petticoat Lane in popularity.

Spitalfields Market

One of the main attractions of the market is the sheer range of stalls that congregate under its roof on a Sunday. At the front of the market (towards Commercial Street) there's a cluster of stalls selling organic fruit and veg, meat, breads and pastries, organic fruit juice and more unusual things like fresh tofu and homemade Jamaican sweets. There are now a multitude of interesting clothing stalls scattered throughout the market selling anything from retro classics (shirts from £8, jackets from around £25) to new fashion from young designers. The simple wrap-around skirts for £25 were a good deal as was the thick wool overcoat recently found here for £18. For those interested in more intellectual pursuits there are several very good second-hand book stalls selling quality paperback fiction for around £3 and Magpie Bookshop can be found towards the back of the market. Spitalfields is also a good place to find things for the home from small items like a designer soap tray to large things like a stainless steel filing cabinet for £150. The two furniture stalls towards the back of the market usually have some interesting pieces of reconditioned second-hand furniture and a small gallery space has been set up in this area, where local artists sell their work.

Spitalfields is an excellent place to shop for quality toys, gifts and knick knacks. As well as the stalls offering such things there are several long-established gifts shops with stock to rival most of the posh shops in Islington, but usually a little cheaper. The main shops to look out for are House of Bohemia at the front of the market and In on the side of the market.

Refreshments, too, are well catered for at Spitalfields. Take the weight off your feet and admire your new purchases over a cappuccino at Spitz Café (one of my favourites) or snack at one of the many food stalls at the front of the market that offer everything from Tex-Mex to Thai. If you have a sweet tooth try the German bakery stall at the back of the market which has a great selection of freshly made Teutonic pastries to choose from.

Although the Sunday Market has become a great success attracting huge crowds, one or two recent changes are not so welcome. The wonderful Heath Robinson-style clock sculpture and

160

miniature children's railway that used to take pride of place within the building have both been closed and increases in stall rent have meant that one or two of the interesting junk stalls have stopped trading. In the longer term there are still plans to sell and redevelop the back of the market into a merchant bank; thankfully the front half of the building is listed. Let's hope this wonderful market doesn't become a victim of its own success or the ambitions of City developers.

Getting a Stall

The popularity of the market has meant a considerable increase in the price of a stall here, so that prices are now comparable to Camden or Portobello Market. If you're interested phone Spitalfields Development Group on 020 7377 1496.

STRUTTON GROUND, SW1

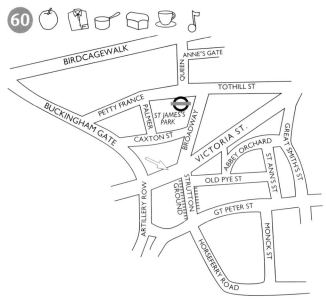

Strutton Ground (the south side of Victoria Street)
Tube: *St James's Park (Circle, District)*
Buses: *11, 24, 211, 507*
Open: *Monday-Friday 11.30am-3pm*

Strutton Ground is a small lunch-time market in the heart of Victoria. Every weekday around thirty stalls set up here and await the rush of office workers during the lunch hour. If you don't like crowds it's a good idea to visit this market either before 12 noon or after 2pm. The market offers high quality but basic fruit and veg, cut flowers, cheap videos and CD's, good value office clothing for women with suits starting from £25, and a stall selling a jumble of kids' clothes out of cardboard boxes for between £1 and £4. There are also several stalls selling fashionable shoes for between £3.99 and £12.99, and an excellent chocolate stall offering two large bars of Milka swiss chocolate for £1, and boxes of Baci chocolate for

£3. There's also a stall dealing in brand-name cosmetics for well below high street prices that is always surrounded by women on the hunt for a bargain. There are several mixed stalls on the market with one selling underwear and sunglasses, and another offering bags, belts and batteries at very reasonable prices. On a recent visit, the tinkle of breaking glass drew a small crowd to a demonstration of the "Eurotool" which was great fun although few waited long enough to delve into their pockets.

Being a lunch-time market, there are no end of places to get a drink or a bite to eat. Among the best are The Trio Bar for basic food, Finnegan's Wake public house for a pint, Greens for take-away wholefood, Stiles bakery and the more fancy Le Pain du Jour. At the top end of the market is the long established Laughing Halibut for traditional fish and chips as well as the Express Coffee Co. which does good coffee but is short of seating. If the market cafés are too busy, try Café Bianco just around the corner on Greycoat Place.

Getting a Stall
For further details contact Westminster Council (see appendix).

SWISS COTTAGE, NW3

In the middle of the site between Avenue Road and Winchester Road.
Tube: *Swiss Cottage (Jubilee line)*
British Rail: *South Hampstead*
Buses: *13, 46, 82, 113, 268 (Avenue Road);*
C11, C12, 31 (Adelaide Road)
Open: *Friday, Saturday (busiest day) & Sunday 8am-5.30pm*
Wednesday 10am-2pm (Farmers Market)

A rare example of a sixties development with a beating heart, Swiss Cottage market is awash with undiluted community spirit. Stashed behind slicing arterial roads, this relaxed market is a real find for newcomers, with a great range of goods and a refreshingly non-commercial atmosphere. Browsing round the leafy square you see both the professional and the amateur, but all stallholders are very friendly and, mostly, willing to barter. The best things about the market are the new and second-hand clothes, and the books. Sartorial bargains abound with designer label cast-offs going for outstanding prices, and plenty of cheap first-hand and occasional retro items; the jewellery is also good. The book stalls (particularly the one nearest the library, which also does cheap CDs) offer both classic and off-beat selections of fiction and brain fodder, as well as brand-new titles at reduced prices. Other stalls sell a mixture of plants and flowers, candles and aromatherapy oils, carpets, fruit and veg, accessories, haberdashery, bric-à-brac and antiques, household and electrical goods.

The model community centre next door to the market dishes up hot and cold food all week, and has a small outdoor eating area which fills up with a real pick 'n' mix of people most days. Further afield is the Swiss Cottage pub for Alpine kitsch and a pint, or Louis Hungarian Confectioners 5 mins away at No.12 Finchley Road, where twiddly cakes can be consumed in a period sixties setting complete with column fish tank and (if you're lucky) live piano music. A park, a swimming pool and a sixties library also share the site with the market. The library is well worth a look for its period piece interior, whose modernist light-flooded spaces house one of London's best collections of psychology and philosophy books.

Getting a stall

The market is privately run (with profits funding charity projects). For further details contact market manager, Odarkwei on 0831 354 143 or 020 7586 8731.

TACHBROOK STREET, SW1

Tachbrook Street between Warwick Way and Churton Street
Tube: *Pimlico (Victoria), Victoria (Victoria, District and Circle)*
Buses: *11, 211, 239, C1, C10*
Open: *Monday-Saturday 9.30am-4.30pm*

Tachbrook Street Market has seen much better days in its long history dating back to the 19th century. It has now dwindled to just half a dozen stalls selling quality fruit and veg, cut flowers and fresh fish. There have been some encouraging changes in recent years with the arrival of a stall specialising in olives and olive oil and another dealing in second-hand furniture and knick-knacks, but the market seems unlikely to develop much further with the local Tescos just around the corner.

Despite the subdued nature of the market, the area is still very much worth a visit if only to escape the polluted and crowded mayhem around Victoria station. If you like hunting for second-hand bargains there are three excellent charity shops in the area: FARA on Tachbrook Street, Oxfam on Warwick Way and the wonderful Crusade on Upper Tachbrook Street. If you're feeling peckish I strongly recommend a piece of pizza and a cappuccino at Gastronomia Italia, on Upper Tachbrook Street, which also has tables outside on fine days.

Getting a stall
For further details contact Westminster Council (see appendix).

Tachbrook Street

WALTHAMSTOW, E17

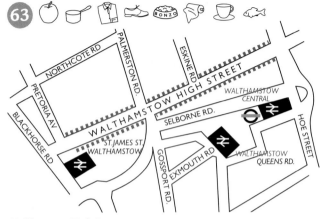

Walthamstow High Street
Tube/BR: *Walthamstow Central (Victoria)*
Buses: *W17, 212, 20, 34, 48, 58, 69,*
212, 215, 257, 275, W11, W15
Open: *Monday-Saturday 9am-5pm*

Many locals claim that this is the longest market in Britain, which is
probably an exaggeration given the size of Portobello Market (see
page 131), but it is certainly quite a trek from St James Street to the
end of the market at Hoe Street. Many local markets are now facing
difficulties with the ascension of the supermarket, but Walthamstow
is a rare and wonderful exception. There are many reasons for
Walthamstow's continued success among them the fact that the
wide thoroughfare of Walthamstow High Street has been pedestrianised, making it a natural focal point, as well as a great place for
shopping and strolling. The shops in the area compliment the
market rather than compete with it, with some excellent butchers,
fish mongers and continental food shops. Another draw are the six
charity shops that line its route, beginning with one of London's
largest Oxfam shops on the junction with St James Street.

There are about 500 stalls lining the half mile route of the market selling all manner of things. The stall selling large white bath towels for £4 each was good value, and there are numerous cheap shoe stalls with one of the best situated towards the Hoe Street end of the market selling fashionable women's shoes for between £5 and £25. Although the clothing stalls are not as trendy as those at a market like Camden, there are plenty of stalls selling street fashion at keen prices. The one selling remainder and slight seconds from major high street shops for £5 a garment was particularly good value. Walthamstow also has lots of cheap T-shirt and underwear stalls with offers like three pairs of cotton underpants for £5. Among the many fabric stalls on the market there's a particularly good one on the junction with Palmerston Road offering quality curtain fabric for as little as £3.99 per metre; and another further along sells Asian and African fabric at very low prices. There are some superb fruit and veg stalls with one selling huge carrier bags of seedless grapes for only £1 and another offering 5lb of Desirée potatoes for the same price. Walthamstow used to have a very limited range of fruit and veg, but there has been an increase in diversity in recent years and what you can't find on the market can always be found at other food stores along the route. Likewise, the H. Clare stall has been selling quality fresh fish here for umpteen years, but only the basics, for more unusual fish try the fishmongers opposite.

Unusual stalls at Walthamstow market include the country and western stall selling CD's covering every aspect of the genre from standing by your man to leaving him with four hungry children and a crop in the field. There's also a very good aromatherapy stall with scents to relax or stimulate you for only £1.50 per bottle. The market also has two stalls where the name of "Dyson" is mud, trading as they do in Hoover bags and accessories. For romantics who would rather return to their loved one with flowers than vacuum cleaner accessories, there are several stalls selling cut flowers and one dealing in cheap bedding plants.

If you manage to walk the length Walthamstow market on a busy day you will need some refreshment on the way. Among the best places to find good British food is The Waltham Stove,

Duncombes Cockney Diner, L.Manze pie and mash shop, Doobry's Sandwich Bar and the Fishnet for fish and chips. If you don't mind eating on the move there are food stalls a-plenty after Palmerston Road including the long established Tubby Isaacs sea food stall, Mel's West Indian take-away and the very popular Indian food stall.

Walthamstow is an ideal market to visit if you want to see a neighbourhood market still in its prime. Unlike many local markets it's busy and interesting even on a weekday. A good way to approach the market is through the wonderful Springfield Park and Walthamstow Nature Reserve which will take about 45 minutes, but gives you a great dose of nature before the hussle and bustle of the market.

Getting a Stall

For further details contact:
Trading Standards Office
8 Buxton Road
Walthamstow E17
020 8520 4071

WELL STREET, E9

Well Street from Morning Lane to Valentine Road
BR: *Hackney Downs (Liverpool Street),*
Hackney Central (Broad Street)
Buses: *26, 277, 333, 26, 30*
Open: *Monday-Saturday 9.30am-4pm*

The founder of Tesco supermarket, Jack Cohen, had a stall here over seventy years ago so it's only fitting that the Tesco store at the top end of the market takes most of the local trade today. These days there are only a few stalls here during the week and about ten stalls on Saturdays selling fruit and veg as well as cheap and basic clothing. The traditional pie and eel shop, quality butchers and excellent bicycle repair shop make this an interesting street, but one not worth venturing too far to visit.

Getting a Stall
For further details contact Hackney Council (see appendix).

171

WEMBLEY SUNDAY MARKET, HA9

Car park between Olympic Way and First Way
(north side of Wembley Stadium)
Tube: *Wembley Park (Metropolitan Line)*
BR: *Wembley Stadium*
Buses: *83, 92, 182, 204, 224, 18, 224*
Open: *Sunday 9am-2pm*

Despite its dramatic location beneath the flank of Wembley
Stadium, this certainly isn't a market in the premier league. It's got
size: on a sunny day the stalls spread right across a large car park –
and character: juddering generators, good-humoured shoppers, the
smell of doughnut fat, lively stallholders and the pulse of musical
tasters from the CD stalls all make for a fairground atmosphere; but
it's still got the feel of being very much a locals-only market. And
punters come in droves, happy to spend a few hours on a Sunday
morning having a wander and looking at massed ranks of bargain
market classics ranging from pet food to plugs.

172

Although it's probably not worth a special journey, what Wembley Market does have in its favour is choice: if one fleece jacket isn't quite what you want, there are around thirty other stalls which can sell you an alternative. Clothes in general are better than average, with the high street seconds/copies stalls offering good buys: trendy quilted coats for only £15, or more substantial wool jackets for £25; plus there are plenty of more unusual examples of (predominantly girls') fashion separates at low-commitment prices, and towards the middle of the market, lots of shirts, jeans, jackets, sportswear, shoes and trainers.

As usual with a local market, utility goods make up the bulk of the merchandise. Tides of functional bedding, throws (some nice Moroccan-style sofa covers for £10), pillows, towels, dishcloths, cheap electronic items (miked-up 'auctioneers' are dotted throughout the market, trying to bait an audience with £1 stereos and threadbare banter), tools, bags, purses and dumpbins of miscellaneous 50p wonders wash all round the market. But slotted in amongst all this, the odd outcrop of idiosyncrasy does manage to thrive, particularly in the form of Indian food stalls which dish up steaming fresh naan breads and spitting kebab sticks - a more palatable option than the old-school greasy options on offer from the mobile van brigade. A few cheap music stalls also buck the '101 Opera Anthems' trend of many local markets, doing a good line in both chart and back catalogue albums (predominantly dance, swing and soul), with some providing decks to try out their more obscure vinyl.

Parking isn't cheap (around £6), so if you do feel the urge to visit Wembley Market from a distance, you're probably better off sticking to public transport - the walk from Wembley Park tube is only five minutes.

Getting a Stall

For further details about getting a stall contact John Fowler on 017268 17809

WESTMORELAND STREET, SE17

On Westmoreland Street, off the Walworth Road, a few minutes south of the East Street turn off.

Tube: *Elephant & Castle (Northern, Bakerloo)*

Buses: *(Walworth Road) 12, 35, 40, 45, 68, 171, 176, 468, X68*

Open: *Monday-Saturday 9am-4pm, Sundays 8am-1pm (Bric-à-Brac)*

During the week Westmoreland Road definitely plays second fiddle to East Street market five minutes away, with only a handful of stalls selling fruit and veg, household essentials, cheap clothes and food to the odd passer-by. But on Sundays, the market really comes into its own when it expands to fill the entire length of the road down to Queen's Row as well as a section of Horsley Street with stalls and pitches selling junk and bric-à-brac; by midday the street is buzzing with a chatty mixture of locals from the surrounding estates and visitors from further afield all on the lookout for a serious bargain. And there are plenty to be had amongst the tidal wave of clobber and clothes, much of which is just dumped in piles on the pavement, or spills out of vans, old prams or boxes – the shambolic presentation means prices are very low, so there are plenty of 50p wonders to be had if you are prepared to get stuck in.

A lot of the stuff on offer is sub-jumble junk, with broken and dirty casualties from decades past lined up with larger items like fridges, stereos and furniture, but a few stall holders seem to have weeded out the rubbish and stock some attractive and unusual retro knick-knacks and ephemera, like cocktail glasses, jewellery, clocks and frames – mostly going for less than a fiver.

Household items, such as old cutlery, pans and crockery, are also worth a look, as are the numerous book sections on many of the stalls – amongst the many dentist's surgery-style reads are a few more recent titles going for next to nothing, plus the occassional choice buy for fans of period-piece graphics. A handful of stalls sell cheap copy trainers, shoes, new shirts and trousers, but predominantly clothes are second-hand with rails of 50p and £1 items everywhere; although some may throw up the odd find, this is not likely to be the best hunting ground for retro purists. Music, though, is everywhere, with CDs, records and tape stocks including some good bargains: new CDs go for an impressive £6 to £8 for contemporary back catalogue titles on one stall, and in boxes of old albums there is often more on offer than just pop deadwood from the eighties. Once you've trawled through this enormous pick 'n' mix, stop for a pint at The Bricklayers Arms at the end of the road, or pop into Arment Eels and Pies for some traditional stodge.

Getting a Stall
For further details contact Southwark Council (see appendix).

Bargains & Banter

Find a bargain in an East London street market.
It's not just shopping, it's entertainment.

Petticoat Lane
London's most famous street market

Columbia Road Flower Market
happy gardening starts here

Brick Lane Market
home of bric-a-brac

Whitechapel Road Market
fruit & spice & everything nice!

The four markets are within easy walking distance of each other.
See the entries in this guide for details of
opening hours.

Cityside

TOWER HAMLETS

east London markets
come and be part of the fun!

WHITECHAPEL, E1

North side of Whitechapel
from Vallance Road to Brady Street
Tube: *Whitechapel (Metropolitan, District)*
Buses: *25, 253*
Open: *Monday-Saturday 8.30am-5.30pm*
Thursday 8.30am-1pm

Whitechapel market has a long history dating back to the 17th
century. In Victorian times most of the traders were Irish and Jewish
immigrants to the East End. Both communities have now largely
left the area and their place has been taken by the Bangladeshi
community that has now established itself in Whitechapel. Blooms
restaurant at no.90 was one of the last remaining legacies of the
market's Jewish past, but that closed in the mid nineties to make
way for a fast-food outlet. The memorial to Edward VII erected by
the Jewish community of East London in 1911, which stands opposite the Royal London hospital, gives some indication of the area's
past.

The market is still a popular place to shop for the local
community and there is a reasonable range of goods among the fifty

or so stalls that do business here. There are several cheap stalls selling material by the yard, some of which have interesting Asian fabrics. The clothes stalls are pretty mixed with lots of cheap but frumpy garments, but also some excellent fashion items at knock-down prices. Among the recent bargains found here were Gap canvas baggy trousers for £20 and some well made silk shirts for £9.99. Likewise, most of the shoes available are pretty awful, but one stall has some trendy styles, including fashionable women's sandals for only £11.99. Other items on offer include small electrical goods, haberdashery, bags, kids clothes and toys, fresh fish, fruit and veg (both basic and exotic) and a stall selling good-value kitchen equipment.

Whitechapel is a good place to visit if you want to see a friendly neighbourhood market that is still thriving and popular with locals. London's East End is also a great place to wander with the Whitechapel Gallery to the west and Brick Lane with its new cafes and established Indian restaurants just a short walk away. If you fancy refreshment closer to the market try Taja, at the begining of the market, which serves excellent Indian food in a building that used to be a public toilet.

Getting a stall
For further details contact Tower Hamlets Council (see appendix).

Whitechapel

WHITECROSS STREET, EC1

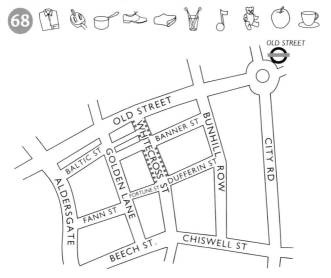

Whitecross Street, between Old Street and Errol Street.
Tube: *Old Street (Northern); Barbican (Metropolitan and Circle)*
Buses: *55, 243, 505 (Old Street)*
BR: *Old Street*
Open: *Monday-Friday 10am-2.30pm*

Whitecross Street is a local cut-through between funky, but slightly
shabby, Old Street and City-slick Moorgate that runs between
blocks of public housing to end up beneath the impressive skyline
geometry of the Barbican Towers. Its lively lunchtime market
reflects these distinct districts with a mixed trade of locals, intermit-
tent trendies and office workers wandering north in search of a
bargain – by one o'clock the street's many pubs and cafés are
flooded with white and blue shirts. What it has lost in terms of size
over the years (there are now a number of bald patches in the line
of stalls), the market seems to make up for in lunch-hour bustle.

Although Whitecross Street is primarily a no-frills, functional market selling standard stuff, it's a good spot for cheap (predominantly women's) clothes – the sheer number of stalls means there are lots of decent bargains: gingham blouses for £3, dresses for £10, suits for under £50. A few traders specialise in more fashionable ranges, but core stock is understated smart/casual suits, trousers, dresses and skirts, with the odd name brand popping up at significantly reduced prices. Men's shirts and T-shirts, kids clothes, shoes and general sportswear also make an appearance, dotted amongst blocks of discount socks and undies. Cherry Tree Walk at the south end of the market offers more of the same, plus handbags for under a fiver and good deals on bedding and luggage.

Other stalls sell flowers and plants, fruit and veg, household goods, toiletries, cheap books and mags (pick up back issues of anything from The Economist to Esquire for 50p each), sweets, jewellery, toys, and CDs and tapes – Whitecross Street has a number of discount music stores, so make sure you shop around before you commit yourself. Single-range stalls also offer multiple choice on goods ranging from sunglasses to cyber-pets.

As well as being home to a string of cafés, chippies and take-aways, Whitecross Street stashes away a few upmarket eateries: Carnevale, an award-winning vegetarian restaurant serving hot and cold food to eat in or take-away, does seriously tempting mains (e.g. sweet potato frittata) and delicious desserts; Tassili (on the right, just off the main road on Roscoe Street) serves up Mediterranean-style lunches and snacks; and Baracca has real Italian set lunches at reasonable prices. Alternatively, buy some take-away, head back up to Old Street, cross the road and sit and eat lunch in the grounds of the ruined church.

Getting a stall
For further details contact Islington Council (see appendix).

WOOLWICH & PLUMSTEAD MARKET, SE18

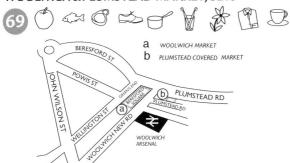

a WOOLWICH MARKET
b PLUMSTEAD COVERED MARKET

Woolwich Market
Beresford Square, Woolwich.
BR: *Woolwich Arsenal (London Bridge); (or take the ferry south across the Thames from Woolwich North (North London Line)).*
Buses: *(Beresford Street) 51, 96, 99, 244, 291, 422*
Open: *Monday-Saturday 9am-5pm, Thursday 9am-2pm*

Downstream from the Thames Barrier and easily eclipsed by the more glamourous and intact attractions of near neighbour Greenwich, Woolwich feels like a place nudged just outside the radar of central London's interest. Historically, Woolwich played an essential role in the capital's economy as the home of both the Royal Dockyard and Royal Arsenal, but now those industries have gone (the first in the 1860's, the second after the last war) it feels like somewhere resigned to being just another slice of inner suburbia.

Woolwich Market (setting up under the Arsenal Gate in Beresford Square since well before the turn of the century), does something to break up the slightly anonymous town centre with a lively range of functional and frivolous goods aimed mainly at the local population. Essentially operating as a standard provisions market with a contingent of clothes stalls, Woolwich holds few surprises and as such is probably not worth a lengthy trip.

That said, if you live at all locally or just happen to be in the area, the market does offer excellent fruit and vegetables. As you

181

enter the market from the Woolwich New Road, an impressive spread of traditional greens and predominantly British fruits (beansprouts is about as exotic as it gets here) opens out along a triangle of stalls – load up everything for a stew or salad for just a few pounds. Stall holders are friendly and willing to offer advice: the market is very much a focus for Woolwich's many different local communities so the atmosphere is one of good-humoured tolerance. There is also a shellfish stall well-stocked with classic fishy nibbles and mounds of vivid pink shrimps and crab sticks, sold by the cup.

The remainder of the square's stalls are made up of street-market standards, household goods and toiletries, cheap clothes (some of the more fashionable stalls might have the occassional bargain amongst the racks of crackling acrylic, but the emphasis is definitely on selling to teens with firm flesh to bare!), shoes, carpets, toys and computer games, children's clothes, brand-a-like sportswear, football kits, pet food, hair accessories and jewellery, bags and luggage, bedding and underwear. Stand-out specialisms are the Indian incense and body-art stall, which offers low commitment henna tattoos (the Nike tick icon is popular for £2.99) and cheap burning oils; the man both selling and sewing cheap footballs; and The Music Man, who blasts out Polyfilla tunes of high drama and heartbreak across the market: if your favourite act don't wear cable knits then it's probably best to give his CD stall a wide berth. Woolwich also has great flowers, with a number of stalls offering very tempting prices on both traditional and more exotic blooms, e.g. a large bunch of sunflowers for £1.50. The material and haberdashery stalls also benefit from a bit of competition, with yards of cloth going for as little as £1.

There are a number of friendly greasy spoon cafés round the perimeter of the market, but if you fancy something a bit more substantial, Woolwich New Road offers a choice of three very different cuisines: the Ordnance pub does Mediterranean-style grills; Tai Tip Mein serves Chinese lunches for under a fiver; and for traditionalists, there is Kenroy's Pie & Eel shop.

Plumstead Market
Plumstead Road
(round corner from Woolwich Market)
Details as above.

70

A minute's walk from Woolwich Market is Plumstead Covered Market. The short route between the two sites doesn't promise much: the pavement is flanked with yet more cheap clothes, brand-a-like trainers and other low-impact bargains. The handful of stalls which make up the market itself occupy just the front section of a grand thirties steel frame warehouse which lies opposite the now defunct Royal Arsenal buildings – the strong sense of departed history makes for a decidedly half-hearted atmosphere. Traders house their goods in attractive beach hut-style cabins, but an apparent lack of interest in presentation means that a lot of stock is just plonked in boxes or on trestles. That said, there are a few specialists tucked away in Plumstead Market whose stalls are model examples of the art of organised cramming: in the far corner, one sells fishing rods and equipment, nearer the front another stocks everything for the keen dart player – from arrows to D.I.Y. trophies.

Other things on offer are both second-hand and cheap new clothes, furniture, underwear, material and a range of bric-à-brac and junk which doesn't promise many 50p wonders. The best thing about Plumstead Market is the cheap books. There are a number of book sections in which good modern titles are dotted amongst the saccharine battalions of Mills & Boon. The Book Browser (the first stall on the far left as you enter) is a small but well-stocked "proper" book stall, which is particularly good for older editions of classic fiction and non-fiction (orange and blue Penguins go from £1), and for well-priced and attractive collectables.

Getting a Stall
For further details about a stall at either Woolwich or Plumstead Market contact Greenwich Council (see appendix).

APPENDIX

Listed below are all the relevant council addresses if you're interested in trading at a council run market:

Camden Council
Environmental Department
Consumer Protection Services
Camden Town Hall
Argyle Street
WC1H 8EQ
020 7974 6939/6917

Greenwich Council
Public Services
11th Floor Riverside House
Woolwich High Street
SE18 6DN
020 8921 5835

London Borough of Hackney
Borough Services
Integrated Civil
Engineering Service
Rossington Street
E5 8SP
020 8356 3327/3367/3702

London Borough of Hammersmith and Fulham
Environmental Protection
Division
Town Hall Extension,
5th Floor
King Street
W6 9ZY
020 8748 3020 X4977

Islington Council
Regulatory and Planning
Services
Consumer Protection Division
Street Trading Section
157–167 Upper Street
N1 1RE
020 7477 3830 (Mrs Dervish)

Kensington and Chelsea
Market Office
72 Tavistock Road
W11 1A
020 7727 7684

Lambeth Council
Market Trading
53 Brixton Station Road
SW9 8PQ
020 7926 2530

Lewisham Council
(for Catford, Lewisham and
Deptford Markets)
Street Trading Sector
3rd Floor
Town Hall Chambers
Rushey Green
Catford
SE6 4RY
020 8314 7111

Newham Council
Land and Property Services
455 Barking Road
East Ham
E6 2LN
020 8472 1450 ext 47611

Southwark Council
Street Trading and Enforcement
SAST House
Dawes Street
SE17 1EL
020 7 277 4597

Tower Hamlets
Market Service
29 Commercial Street
E1 0AU
020 7 377 8963

Wandsworth Council
Markets Department
Room 59, Town Hall
Wandsworth High Street
SW18 2PU
020 8871 6382

Westminster City Council
9th Floor
Markets Department
City Hall
Victoria Street
SW1E 6QP
020 7641 6000 (Mr Byron)

Listed below are other useful
addresses for insurance and
display equipment:

**The National Market
Trader's Federation**
Hampton House
Hawshaw Lane
Hoyland
Barnsley
South Yorkshire
S74 0HA
01226 7490211

Shopfittings Direct
428 Whippendell Road
Watford
WD1 2PT
01923 232425

Order Form

The following titles are also available from Metro Publications:

Museums & Galleries of London
Abigail Willis
£8.99

Book Lover's London
Leslie Reader
£7.99

Food Lovers' London (2nd Edition)
Jenny Linford
£6.99

A Taste of London
Jenny Linford
£6.99

Veggie London (2nd Edition)
Craig Wilson & Veronica Wheatley
£6.99

The London Market Guide (2nd Edition)
Andrew Kershman & Ally Ireson
£5.99

Bargain Hunters' London
Andrew Kershman
£5.99

Gay London
Graham Parker
£6.99

Visiting Greenwich & The Dome
Sarah Leese
£4.99

Please send your order along with a cheque made payable to Metro Publications to the address below.
Postage is free, please allow 14 days for delivery.

Metro Publications,
PO Box 6336, London N1 6PY
e-mail: metro@dircon.co.uk
www.metropublications.com